THE EARLY INDUS CIVILISATION

Hunting to Farming

THE EARLY INDUS CIVILISATION

Hunting to Farming

Madhusudan Mishra

SHIPRA

ISBN : 81-7541-286-0

First Published in India in 2006

The Early Indus Civilisation: Hunting to Farming

Published by:
SHIPRA PUBLICATIONS
115-A, Vikas Marg, Shakarpur Delhi-110092, INDIA
Phone: 91-11-55277210, 91-11-22500954
Fax: 91-11-22458662
E-mail: info@shiprapublications.com
www.shiprapublications.com

Preface

In the present work I have been able to corroborate some views of the archaeologists with some texts of the Indus inscriptions. If the language is at the isolating stage, the Indus Civilisation too, reflecting through the texts, is at its very infancy. It has just gone from hunting to farming. But then it does not match properly with the ruins of the cities uncovered through excavations.

For many years I did not have any answer for the absence of the records in the advanced stage of the language, and every now and then I regretted miserably. Now I could find it and narrated the same in the introductory chapter.

My research on Indus started with the little book From Indus to Sanskrit Part I (1996), and it was followed by Part II (1997) and Part III (1998). In 1999, a number of independent articles on the same subject appeared with the title THE DISCOVERY OF INDUS. In 2000, the evolution of THE INDUS LANGUAGE and its transition into Sanskrit was published. My research had a pulsating march towards success in decipherment. The earlier views were often ruthlessly crushed by myself and new ones were proposed, and these too had often the same fate.

My next book The Ṛgveda In The Indus Inscriptions (2003) and later The Indus Aryans and the Vedic Culture (2004) are able to face the criticism of the most straightforward critics. One of my friends once made a very sincere remark about my research on Indus: Had you been on a wrong track, you could not have travelled this long distance. I also realise that I have travelled on a right track and I also see a bright path ahead. The goal is still farther away.

Mahāṣṭamī
11.10.2005

Madhusudan Mishra

Contents

1

Introduction

The History group of the Children's Encyclopaedia founded by Sir Arthur Mee briefly describes the march of Man from the age of Barbarism to the United Nations. The first two chapters of the group are very relevant to this introduction.

The texts of the Indus inscriptions, as far as read and understood, are in the form of hotch-potch. I have been able to arrange the contents of the texts as briefly suggested by the author of the history group of the Encyclopaedia. The first group of texts relates to their nomadic life; the second group relates to their village-life; and the third group relates to a time when they had forgotten the past sufferings.

The texts of the Indus inscriptions are the earliest thoughts and experiences of that 'creature which had a mind'. The historian of the Encyclopaedia has hastily come to the language of that primitive community, but does not say how it arose. It is from here that I proceed to say something.

The primitive human beings too bellowed like animals. Their utterance consisted of resonants, initially only the vowels, forming the triangle of u i a in the diagram of the cardinal vowels. When these vowels came to a measurable length, they consisted of the socalled three mātrās: ū3 ī3 ā3. But when these too came down to two mātrās (ū ī ā) and then to just one mātrā (u i a), that is, when these vowels could be distinguished as short and long, it was the beginning of the human speech. The three mātrāic vowels too were uttered by the human beings, but only when somebody was called from a distance. A longer vowel could be no more than the animal's cry. That is why, when two similar long vowels met, they just merged together without increase in mātrā.

The vowels u i, short and long, also later climbed down to o e of the diagram, and the lowest a combined with the highest u i to make diphthongs. Thus the following were the vowels at the beginning of the human speech: u ū i ī a ā o ō e ē au ai āu āi.

These vowels were later preceded by the soft and hard breathings (h ẖ), hissing sounds (ṣ s ś) and nasals (ñ m ṅ ṇ n). The fricatives v y were born from u i when some dissimilar vowels immediately followed them. The stops of various series, voiceless and voiced as well as aspirates and unaspirates, were also born later.

At the beginning of this human speech nearly 500 syllables were there. These comprised the limited vocabulary of those primitive people: They saw a turtle going slowly and said: ka 'it goes slowly'. Later, the turtle itself was called ka. They saw a fish swimming and said: ma 'it swims'. The fish itself was later named ma. They saw a river flowing and said: na 'it flows'. This river itself was called na. They saw another river flowing with indistinct noise and they added one more syllable: na-da 'it flows and makes indistinct noise'. This river itself was later called nada. It is remarkable that the verb was conceived first, then the noun, and not vice versa.

These speaking human beings were still nomads. They lived on hunting and gathering food and clothing materials. The formation of the word grāma (grā 'wandering' + ma 'end') suggests that they stopped wandering, which was the beginning of the founding of the 'villages'. But then they continued to suffer due to lack of a shelter. This suffering (da) too came to an end (ma) when they built da-ma (house). We see their advancing civilisation through the words then formed.

When the villages were founded and houses were built, they began to domesticate the useful animals. Their observation, gā 'goes' va 'into the stable' at some advanced stage of the domestication of the milch cattle shows that 'cows' were the first to be domesticated. The Sanskrit tradition knew it very well, because go 'cow' is derived thus: gacchatīti gauḥ (a cow is so called because she goes into the stable). We realise how the IE for COW is a hoax. Their observation of the natural phenomena too is very remarkable. They saw the night approaching and said: ṇa ga (the light is going, that is, the darkness is coming). The oldest Vedic word for 'night' is nág (used only once in the RV). The river, later called Saras-vat-ī, was mightily flowing before them. But they were not able to name it. They simply observed: ṣa ra ṣa (it flows from the mountain and stops). Later sáras 'pond' formed by the held up water at some points of depression in the bed of the river, gave it the name saras-vat-ī 'abounding in ponds'. We can thus imagine the level of their civilisation at the isolating stage of the language.

At so early stage in their life, they began to give written form to their grammarless language. As the words were monosyllabic and they stood for certain animals, birds, insects and physical objects, they portrayed them to represent those syllables. They were the most gifted among the primitive people.

Because the groups of people had settled in distant villages, their means of communication were the tiny words engraved on clay-tablets and pieces of bones.

Once they knew how to write their simple language, they recalled all the sufferings of the nomadic life before they settled in villages. However, we do not see them using the past tense, though they use the 'future' and 'order' forms.

In course of wandering they had discovered the fire and also knew how it was differently useful from the water, both offered by the nature itself. They had been watching the changing weathers: if the summer was hot, it was followed by heavy rains; sometimes the rain was in plenty, which also became destructive; sometimes the dry season continued for a longer period; they had also to protect themselves from the sun-stroke. But they waited for the arrival of the rain, which was often predicted by the frogs and other natural events. Sometimes they also experienced a chilly winter.

In course of hunting, they also made small weapons from the bones of the killed animals. While founding villages and building houses, they had to clear off the surroundings from snakes and other harmful creatures.

They had domesticated the cows first of all, which later became the sacred animal in their religious life. They also domesticated horses, which was not an easy affair. Its hindleg was very dangerous. However, they overcame the difficulties, and the horses proved to be their useful animal later.

Ultimately, they were tired of the nomadic life and began founding villages. There are some texts exhorting the people to give up the nomadic life. But it was followed by the coming of the rogue elements like thieves in the villages, against whom they began to employ human guards and domesticated dogs. They invented wheeled carts and flour-mills. They also required fodder for the domesticated cattle. Their house-building had started early, but gradually they made them more comfortable. They discovered oil-lamps for lighting their houses. They had also developed breeding centres for the useful cattle, dug wells for the domestic waters.

Most importantly, they started agriculture. From hunting they came to farming, the important stage of the civilised humanity. They devised reservoirs of waters for irrigation and also dug canals to irrigate the distant lands. In course of farming, they also discovered the intoxicating Soma juice which became the centre of rituals in their later religious life.

This advancement of civilisation has not been recounted through imagination. Everything has been said on the basis of the written documents in the isolating stage of their language.

Unfortunately, the message stops just here. But, archaeologically, there are evidences of the excellent town-planning and other items of the advanced culture. That is not attested by the written documents in the advanced stage of the language.

With the advancement of the Indus society towards urbanised way of life and superior civilisation, the language too should have advanced towards the agglutinative stage with the bisyllabic and longer words in long paragraphs. But the clay-tablets, etc. were unsuitable for this type of language. Thus the messages should have been written on palm-leaves and the barks of the birch-trees, which were perishable materials. When there was some natural catastrophe, these perishable materials were destroyed. That is why, the corresponding documents of the advanced culture did not come down to us.

This language reached the inflexional stage, but the urbanised way of life reverted back to the pastoral stage after the great natural catastrophe. Their academic activities did not stop, but the script used so far was not suitable for that language. Thus their literature became śruti till it was too vast to be stored in memory. They turned to the script then employed for the popular language and fashioned it to agree to its needs.

2

A Long Dry Season

4536  h̲a da, cā ṣa

h̲a (sky) da (heat), cā (dry land) ṣa (embryo)

= (In the) sky (there is) heat; the lands are drying up.

4460 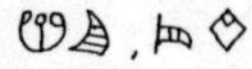 ci ra, h̲a da

ci (long time) ra (speed), h̲a (sky) da (heat)

A long time passed; in the sky there is heat.

These two texts at different places in the compilation have a common theme. They relate to agriculture when it was at very primitive stage.

The first text describes the current situation. The sky is burning and the lands below are drying up. The crops are nearly parched. The second text describes the condition of the nature carried over from the past. It is very hot now, and it is continuing from sometime past.

They had just started farming. The importance of water for the crops was known to them by now. Perhaps they were gradually realising that the monsoon broke at a particular time, and it was getting late. Perhaps canals had not been dug out and the siphoning instrument called ḍhos, mentioned elsewhere, had not been invented, These texts show the anxieties of the people and the administration.

One clause in each text has fossilised as a word in the later phases of the language: cā ṣa has fossilised as cās (cultivable land) in the eastern languages of India. ci ra has fossilised as cira-, used in sg. in various cases in Sanskrit, meaning 'for a long time'. Even h̲a da should have fossilised as the verb sad 'to languish'.

3

The Drying Summer

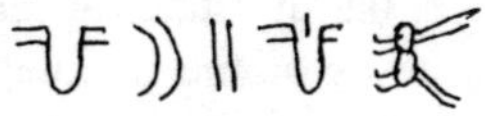

The first part of the text is graphically uncertain. Though the first, the ant-sign, is a c-syllable (identifiable through cī 'ant', extended as cī-ṭī 'the little or black ant'), the vowel following it is not known. On the basis of its geometrical version in another text, it may be read cā. Thus the text appears to be read: cā ṣu ra ṇa ṣa.

The meaning of the first part is already known: if the land is dry ...... The second part ra ṇa ṣa may be supposed to have fossilised as *ráṇas, which is unattested. But ṛṇá 'running away' (as a thief), 'fugitive' RV 6, 12, 5 may be its reduced form. The verb raṇ has a number of deviating meanings: (1) to delight (2) to rattle (3) to go. The different meanings of raṇ must have come through the different shades of the clause in different circumstances: the fire (ra) gives comfort (ṇa), the fire (ra) makes noise (ṇa), the fire (ra) gives life (ṇa), etc.

In order to make the two clauses agree in meaning, which are already syntactically related (ṣu : ṣa), we may propose the following meaning to the second clause: through (the fiery) heat (of the sun) the plants perish. The whole text may say: If the land is dry, the plants perish through the fiery heat of the sun. This is a standing instruction to the farmers not to let the fields get dry.

The text relates to a typically agrarian society, which was totally dependent on nature. Perhaps, by that time, the canals had not been dug and some workable instruments for irrigation were not invented. In some other texts we learn that they had invented a siphoning instrument called ḍhos nowadays.

Just less than fifty years ago in the countryside of India, there was an instrument called ḍhekul in use for siphoning waters from the well. The initial ḍh in ḍhos and ḍhekul indicates their common origin in the primitive society. The Indian people are very faithful to their tradition. In spite of the invention of the modern instruments, the traditional instruments are still in use in the remote countryside.

As we go on reading the Indus texts, we find it just at the beginning of the pastoral culture. The ruins of the urban culture discovered through excavations indicate their later origin, when the language too was at the balmy state of the agglutinative stage. Unfortunately, the documents of the language of the agglutinative stage, written on perishable material like plam-leaves, etc. have been lost to us.

The texts like this had been taken up even earlier, but then it was not possible to give a cogent meaning. Now we have known the language and seen the society with our eyes of imagination. Therefore, we understand what they say.

4

The Coming Hot Summer

ru ksa gha

The reading of the text is hardly doubtful. Because the ligature kṣa is very old, it is taught as one of the basic syllables in the syllabary of the Indian languages individually. These ligatures are three, namely kṣa, tra and jña. The other two also must be present in the Indus syllabary.

In the present text, the last from the right is the future affix, indicating that kṣa is some verbal idea*. Because ru+kṣa combine to become one word in the RV (6, 3, 7), meaning 'shining'** and because ru stands for some fiery object, kṣa may mean 'hot'. The clause 'sun hot-future' seems to mean: the sun will be hot, or, there will be hot sun, or, the coming summer will be very hot.

Perhaps it relates to the weather system in the agrarian Indus society and warns the peasants about the coming drought. The vulgar form of rukṣa in the colloquial dialects is rukh and usually refers to the land which is getting dry or where there is no water.

This text was read exactly as above, but interpreted differently earlier (From Indus to Sanskrit, Pt. II, 1997, p. 51).

---

* The Vedic kṣa (noun) means 'earth' and as verb it means 'to burn'. A further extended form kṣmā too means 'earth'. It appears that all these three are the fossilised forms of the Indus clauses at the isolating stage.

** According to Sāyaṇa, hesitatingly accepted by Geldner, suggesting his own emendation (rūkṣa 'dry'). When it qualifies a bull, rukṣa is more likely to mean 'in heat, sexually excited', corresponding to the fire in flames.

5

The Sun-stroke

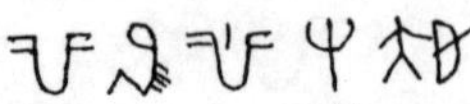

rau ṇa ṣu dhe ṣa

Unless the culture of a prehistoric primitive society is properly known, it is not possible to understand its language. At the early stage of research on the Indus inscriptions, the ideas of the Vedic literature appeared to reflect in them through its fossilised vocables, sharply reduced in size and mutilated semantically. Therefore the clauses, though read almost exactly as now, appeared to give vague meanings, almost of enigmatic nature.

Now when we have realised that the Indus valley civilisation is just the beginning of a human culture and civilisation, when the hunting and gathering had just ended, and farming and agriculture had begun, our understanding of the text is more natural than before.

This small text has two clauses, both syntactically related, indicated by ṣu at the first clause and ṣa at the second.

The syllable rau may be supposed to have fossilised either as lū 'sunstroke' in the modern dialects or as the rarely used 'lao' (the flame of light) colloquially. In both cases, the 'fiery heat' or the 'extreme heat of the sun' is indicated. A farmer was naturally exposed to it, and it was necessary to issue certain warnings against it. Linguistically, the classical ravi 'sun' is not quite different from rau, which has been just extended by -i. The next clause dhe ṣa reflects in the Vedic dhiṣ (used in instrumental: dhiṣ-ā 'mindfully'). Accordingly, the text may be interpreted thus: Because through the heat of the sun (rau) the life (ṇa) perishes (ṣu), be mindful (dhe).

Even at the primitive stage of civilisation, the people were very wise and knew the good and bad aspects of the nature. The clay tablets on which these messages were written were like the pages of a book or individual messages carried to the right persons in the society. In also reveals that there was some administrative machinery working in different fields of the human activities.

6

Plenty of Rain after the Hot Summer

The text probably reads: ra gha dha. If the reading is correct, it may be supposed to have fossilised in Sanskrit as *raktá (through the devoicing and deaspiration of gh and dh).

In Sanskrit, however, rakta (coloured, red, attached, devoted) is said to have been derived from rañj (to please, satisfy), though, on the contrary, raj itself has been deduced from *rakta, which was later extended as raj-ata (silver), raj-an-ī (night). Because silver is a shining object, and night too is generally conceived as bright and star-lit (cf. rā-tr-ī from rā-tṛ 'illuminator'), the root raj means 'to shine'. The classical root rañj is a later creation and the various meanings of rak-ta are later conceptions.

The text ra gha dha may be a clause, ra (fire) gha (sun) dha (brightness) suggesting: the fiery sun shines. Through the phrase stage, the meaning would have been restricted to 'the (fiery) sun', then to 'fiery, red', then to 'coloured', and so on. From this rakta the root raj 'to shine' should have been deduced, which was again extended as raj-ata, raj-anī, rajas, etc. For the root rāj 'to rule over' and the derivative rāj-an 'ruler', we cannot postulate anything other than the strengthening of raj itself. In Sanskrit, rāj also means 'to shine'.

If the order of the last two syllables of the text is changed we have an IE dha gha (fossilised as Swedish Daag, Eng. day, Germ.

Tag, Sansk. ni-dāgha 'summer'), which perhaps means 'the bright sun' being the characteristics of the 'day'.

The first two syllables of the text reflects in the proper noun Raghu, who was a powerful king of the solar dynasty. In the RV, raghú adj. 'running' m. 'runner' betrays the meaning of ra (speed) only, the meaning of ghu being just in imagination. But the second syllable in ṛjú 'straight', conceived through the straight movement of the sun in the sky, should have undergone palatalisation and deaspiration. However, these are the late conceptions of the Vedic age, though the solar (Raghu) dynasty may be as old as the Indus inscriptions.

The original clause in the text of the inscriptions is an observation of nature at the very primitive state of the Indus civilisation. They had observed that when the summer was hot, there was plenty of rain later. It was a guiding indication in respect of agriculture, which had become their main occupation.

7

It Will Rain

A very little clause 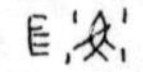 me gha, also followed by  ya ga in the next line elsewhere is remarkable, if the first sign has been correctly read me.

The syllable ma has 'water' as one of the meanings, and me specifically refers to 'rain'. That is to say, me-gha may be supposed to mean: it will rain. Perhaps the whole verbal form has turned up in Sanskrit as the noun megha m. 'the rain-cloud'. It is not an exceptional case. Even the verbal form ṣṭha-gha (will stay) has turned up as sthag 'to stop' in Sanskrit. The participle pra-viṣ-ṭa (entered) has turned up as a new verb pa-i-ṭṭha- (to enter into) in Apabhaṃśa (Hindi pāṭh-).

The next line of the clause me-gha (it will rain), namely ya-ga (action-inj.) perhaps says: do the needful, be active, exploit the situation.

We are at the very early stage of the Indus civilisation. From hunting and gathering, they appear to have come to agriculture. Because they had to depend on monsoon for waters, they were hopefully waiting for its arrival. For them, every natural phenomenon was exciting. It was the wealth of nature which was required to be utilized first of all. The man-made facilities were yet to come. The reservoirs of waters were to be made, the canals had to be dug, and so on.

8

The Arrival of the Rains

4050  bu ci ra

This little text is graphically hardly uncertain, because some texts have been read fairly reliably on the basis of these sound values of the above signs.

Because the ba syllable means 'water' in the lexicons, bu is some state of the waters, probably the rain.

The next two syllables, forming a group, later appears in cira in ciram, cireṇa, cirāya, cirāt, cirasya and cire. If the last syllable ra is a verb, it means 'speed' in the form of 'to come, go, arrive'. From the whole group cira- we suppose that ci is nearly or distantly related with delay.

Now the whole text may be understood to mean: the rains will arrive late. This seems to be some warning for the peasants of the agrarian Indus society.

To trace the fossilised form of this text, we have to go deeper. With the affricate value of /c/, the clause should have fossilised as *busir, from which the verb bus 'to discharge, emit, pour' has been deduced in the Dhātupāṭha.

9

The Fertilising Waters

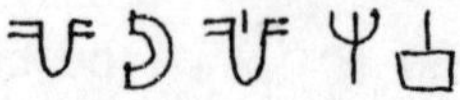

va ṇa ṣu ṇā ṣa

This text has been examined twice earlier (From Indus to Sanskrit, Pt. III, 1998, p. 51 The Indus language, 2000, p. 63). There is no doubt about the meaning of the first part, and it has been examined several times in other contexts when the verb is also not bent towards u.

The second part of the text, ṇā ṣa, may be doubtful about its real sound-value on the first sign and obscure semantically on the whole clause. Taking for granted too that the first sign of this caluse is ṇā, the whole clause is still a riddle. Even the whole text is not a lesser riddle.

Let us start with ṇā ṣa. The traditional lexicons say: ṇa = knowledge, ṣa = wise (and there are other meanings for both of them). If we take them theoretically to their fossilised state, it may be *nās, which actually occurs (RV 2, 39, 6) with its dual form nāsā '(the two holes of the) nose'. Another meaning, however, which has remained unrecorded in any Vedic dictionary, is one which finds itself in the highly controversial and greatly misunderstood anās (RV 5, 29, 10), analysed either as a-nās (noseless) or as an-ās (faceless). These meanings are based on the misconceived ethnology of Vedic India, because such qualities are attributed to Dasyus, who too are wrongly understood.

To understand anās, then also nās and, ultimately, the Indus clause ṇā ṣa properly, we have to decide the exact ethnological status of Dasyu (including Dāsa).

We have to ignore their descriptions in the Vedic Index (Macdonell-Keith). The Avestan Dahyu means 'land and its inhabitants'; the Pehlevi dēh has the same meaning; and the modern Persian dih means 'village', its pl. form dehāt = countryside. Bartholomae could not reconcile the Avestan meaning 'land and its inhabitants' with the then prevalent meaning of the Vedic Dasyu, which deviated widely. In the traditional Sanskrit lexicons of the monosyllabic words, da = mountain and sa (= road, fence) makes us conjecture a meaning like 'village', so that Dahyu literally means 'mountainous village', which may also include its inhabitants. A similar meaning may be given to Dāsa.

As a matter of fact, Dāsas and Dasyus were the members of the same Vedic community, living in the mountainous villages of the countryside, who were dark-skinned on account of working under the hot sun, spoke uncultivated language of the countryside, and had all the bad qualities of the rustic villagers. We can compare the language of the Aśokan inscriptions with the dramatic and canonical Prakrits.

Judged in the context of Dasas and Dasyus, anās may be analysed as a- (devoid of) nās, which requires an X-ray examination agglutinatively regarding its original connotation. Perhaps the meanings, knowledge for ṇa and wise for ṣa of the traditional lexicons reflect in nās, the reduced and fossilised form of ṇā ṣa. These two syllables perhaps mean: know (and) see, because the knowledge is the result of knowing and the wisdom is the result of seeing. Thus the fossilised word nās means 'knowledge and wisdom'. Therefore, a-nās = ignorant and unwise. Two verbs have been used here, because there is difference between knowing and seeing. Saint Kabīr had once retorted to his critics: You say what is written in books; I say what I have seen with my eyes.

The Vedic texts can be better understood through the Indus inscriptions than through comparison with Greek and Latin.

Now the whole text seems to say: Know (and) see that the life comes from the water. These Indus writings show the very infancy of the agrarian life of the Indus people. They had begun to realise the importance of the water not only for their own life but also for the life of the plants and animals.

The verb turning towards u in the first clause is just a syntactical device to connect the following clause. Here the whole clause has become the object of the following verbs.

10

A Torrential Rain in the Evening

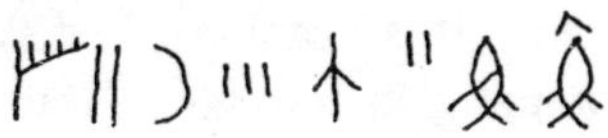

This text had proved to be very obscure in the beginning, but gradually it has given some meaning. The reading is perhaps not at all doubtful: ni ma ẖa gha ta na ra dha. The eight syllables may be equally broken into four clauses: ni ma, ẖa gha, ta na, ra dha. Each of them appear to reflect, at least phonetically, in some Sanskrit vocable: nema, sagh/sah, tán, radh/ṛdh.

Of the several lexical meanings of nema, 'evening' seems to emerge from the following interpretation of the text: ne (day)-ma (past-affix): the day has come to an end (It is evening now). The ne-element in dine (in the day) is an old fossil, di- being the deaspirated form of dhi (light) (cf. dīdhiti 'light'). In Santhali, a noun becomes a verb just by taking a tense-affix: abād (cultivation)-ket-a = cultivated; abād-et-a = cultivates.

The idea of 'being able to bear' in sagh/sah comes through some unpleasant situation. If ẖa (sky) gha (sound) gives the meaning 'the sky thunders', it is supposed to be raining in torrents, which is an unpleasant situation. In later Sanskrit, a 'rainy day' is called dur-dina (a bad day).

The sense of 'continuity' in tán (RV) comes from the cloud raining continuously. The clause ta (womb) na (gem) means: from the cloud the water is pouring down continuously.

If the word-order in the last clause is changed, dhārā means 'the streams of waters'. Here the clause ra (speed) dha (light) simply says: the waters flow in streams.

As there were fewer words than ideas in the language, the same concepts were variously modified to express the intended ideas. We are strained in jumping from one idea to another, but these primitive people easily crossed any barrier. The traditional lexicographers have very carefully designated a central meaning for several distant ideas.

Now we can summarise the whole context. Though the isolating stage of the language is not capable to give a descriptive account of some situation, it has been attempted here: The day has come to an end (ni ma). (It is evening). The sky is thundering (ẖa gha). (It has begun raining in torrents). From the clouds (ta) the waters pour down continuously (na). (The waters) flow (ra) in several streams (dha). (The rays of light conceived as several streams).

It is probably the middle of the rainy season.

An analysis of the context of the text shows that the Indus people at that stage of civilisation were just farmers at the beginning of the agriculture. They watched the nature and used to put up with the hardships caused by it. There is also no doubt that they were gradually becoming poetic in their expression, because it is nature which makes one a poet. We can compare these little clauses with some stanzas of a hymn on Parjanya (5, 83) of the RV: ni ma: -ẖa gha: 1c, 3c, 7, 9. ta na: 6, 10. ra dha: 8b.

Just as there are generally four ideas in an eight-syllabic Anuṣṭubh verse (e.g. āsīd rājā nalo nāma), this Indus text has 4+4 signs representing 4+4 syllables for 4+4 ideas, making a full anuṣṭubh quarter.

A similar text has been interpreted elsewhere: sa ma na nda ḍha bu ṣa (The summer has just ended. The creatures make sweet noise, asking for waters. The frogs bring rain.)

11

The Thunder and Lightning

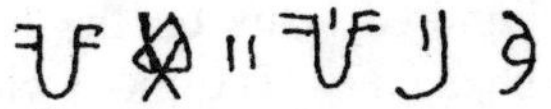

ni nda ṣu ka ṇa ṣa

> (When) in the sky there is the sound of thunder, in the rain-cloud there is the flash of lightning.

The reading of the text is only provisional on the first two signs from the right, but it may prove to be correct in due course. The interpretation, however, may remain provisional for a long time to come. We are not able to identify even a single syllable with exact meaning. Whatever has been proposed in the first instance is based on guess and common sense.

The fitst three syllables from the right reflect in a Sanskrit verb nind 'to censure'. The next three syllables reflect in the verb karṣ/kṛṣ 'to plough' from the intermediate stage *kánas. We may base our interpretation on the late meanings of the fossils (nind: karṣ) of the two clauses. The meanings have jumped like frogs in unpredictable direction.

This is probably the description of the natural phenomenon when it had rained in torrents. As the rain-clouds collided, there was the noise of thunder on the one hand and a flash of lightning on the other. Because the light travels faster than the sound, the former reaches the earth earlier than the sound of the thunder. The Indus people were quick to observe that the agents causing thunder and lightning were the same, but it cannot be said whether they knew that both arose simultaneously.

When we come to the meanings of the fossilised words, 'the sound of thunder in the sky' degenerating into 'censure' is not quite unexpected. But the 'lightning through the rain-cloud' turning into 'ploughing' must have undergone a tortuous journey in the semantic jump. As a matter of fact, the flash of lightning appears to split in several lines, which may have given the impression of a furrowed sky, as if it had undergone ploughing.

Just as the face of a man is distorted in a thick, broken and dirty glass, the Indus clauses have become unimaginably distorted at the third station of their development in the Vedic language.

It is unfortunate that we compress all the developments in the language within few hundred years on the basis of a developing young discipline of archaeology. The Indus clause iti ḥa ā-ṣa of the agglutinative stage was naturalized as iti ha āsa and contracted as itihāsá in Satapatha-Brāhmaṇa. If we could know the age of the clause iti ha āṣa, the time taken in its contraction to itihāsá might be measured. But the fossilization of a clause to a vocable is a different process, the exercise of several millenniums. Unless our sight improves in respect of time-scale, we are liable to finish everything in a short while like the birth, maturity and death of Solomon Grundy in a week.

It is now becoming clear that if we know something definitely about the culture of a community, we can understand its language after it has been read.

12

The Chilly Winter

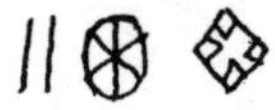

This text appears to be read cī ci ra. With the affricate value of /c/, it may be split as /tśi tśi ra/, and then it seems to reflect in the Vedic vocable śíśira (cold, coolness) AV 6, 55, 2. 12, 1, 36. Later, it is one of the six seasons comprising the months of Māgha and Phālguna, so called because it is the coldest, following the less cold Hemanta and preceding the warm Vasanta (spring). The first vowel, though originally long, has been shortened, probably due to accent on it. Roth connects śíśira with śyā and makes it cognate with śīta (cold).

Even śiva (auspicious) has supposedly evolved from civa in 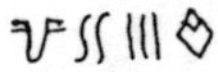 ci (cold) va (water) ra (speed) ṣa (nipple) = cold water runs from the mountain, though the supposed Indus word-order (s+v) may reject this translation. The quoted Indus clause ci va ra ṣa reflects in the Vedic verse: yo vaḥ śivatamo rasaḥ (whatever auspicious liquid you have ......).

If we turn to the interpretation of the Indus clause cī ci ra we may take the final ra (speed) to be the verb. Because the last two syllables reflect in the Vedic cira- (long time), ci ra may be taken to mean: lasts long, goes for a long time. Perhaps cī means summer (though ci means 'cold'), taking the Indian weather system into account. Its fossilization as śíśira phonetically could be predicted, but how the summer turned into cold winter could not be explained. Sometimes the referends jump in the opposite direction.

We can also imagine the state of the Indian civilisation through it. They had just been watching how the different seasons of the year were not alike and of the same duration, though later the whole year was equally divided into six seasons.

13

The Wealth of Nature

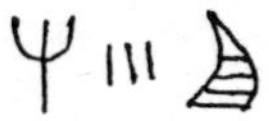

ẖa ta ṇa

The reading of the text is perhaps doubtlessly correct. Its fossilised form in Sanskrit may be *atná, and some atna 'sun' is actually recorded in the traditional Sanskrit lexicons. This atna 'sun' may perhaps give some clue towards the exact meaning of the Indus clause.

The traditional Sanskrit lexicons of the monosyllabic words give specific meanings to these syllables: ha = sky (and a score of other meanings); ta = womb (and some other meanings); and ṇa = knowledge.

In order that these three monosyllabic words could make a sensible clause, we may modify these meanings based on some scientific facts.

The syllable ha may stand for the concept of the whole space, because the meaning 'sky' is just symbolic. Sir Arthur Mee's Children's encyclopaedia, p. 9 says: "If the sun was hollow, over a million balls, each of the size of the earth, could be dropped into it". The syllable ta = womb perhaps refers to this sun. Because ṇa is the basis of the Vedic verb an 'to breathe', it may comprehend the whole concept of 'life'. Thus the clause seems to give a meaning involving space, sun, life. It is the heat and light of the sun which make life possible on the earth. Accordingly, the clause may be understood thus: From the space the sun creates life.

How the whole clause semantically contracted as 'sun' could not have been predicted, though its phonetic transformation was predictable.

In the earlier work "The Ṛgveda in the Indus inscriptions", the same text, though read ẖa ta ṇa as now, was supposed to mean: in the empty space a gem shines, referring to the shining sun. But there being no relevance for this statement, it may be now rejected.

In another text, the central sign reads ṭa, meaning 'earth'. In that case, the meaning of the clause may be the following: the earth is lively through the sky, that is, the heat and light from the sky makes the earth lively.

These inscriptions represent the state of the Indus society just before urbanization, because they were gradually realising the values of the wealth of the nature.

14

The Harmful Aspects of Nature

ri ya va ni ha ṣa ra

This text has ra at the end, which appears to be an affix for pluperfect. Of the remaining six monosyllabic words, the first in each pair may be the subject, the second the verb:

1. ri ya
2. va ni } ra
3. ha ṣa

In a primitive language, the same word is noun at one place and verb at another. Moreover, the subject or object itself has concealed in it the verbal idea appropriate to its original sense. For example, in Santhali, there is a sentence: hako (fish) -ket (past)-ko (pl.)-ā- ko (they) = they fish (pl.)-past, that is, they caught fish. The verbal idea is inherent in the object 'fish' (i.e. they fished). The same may be inherent in the subject also.

Then the three sentences above may give the following meanings:

1. The sun (ri) had (burnt) the crops (ya);
2. The water (va) had (over-flooded) the river (ni); and
3. The wind (ha) had (dried up) the land (ṣa).

That primitive society was watching the activities of the objects of nature. The sun has many good aspects in itself (it keeps warm, gives light, etc.), but it can also destroy the crops. Similarly, the water and wind can be harmful.

Though it was not possible in speech, in writing the pluperfect affix -ra has been made common to all the verbs of the text.

The pluperfect idea (he had gone) may also be conceived as perfect continuous idea (he has been going). Thus the text describes the usual behaviour of the nature: the hot sun has been parching the crops; the flooding rivers have been destroying the crops; and the hot winds have been making the lands dry.

The nature was making them wiser. They would have certainly thought out some plans to overcome the nature.

15

The Weather Forecast

The early phase of the Indus civilisation had an agrarian society. Not long ago, they had given up the nomadic life and had founded villages (grā-ma itself meaning 'cessation of wandering'), building houses for themselves (da-ma itself meaning 'end of hardships'). The village-life gave them security and the houses gave them comfort, leading to prosperity (cf. vardhamānaṃ sve dame 'prospering in their own house' RV 1, 1, 8). They had begun watching the nature very closely, because it could give them comfort without demanding anything in return. Therefore, they did not miss any opportunity provided by the nature.

A text of the Indus inscriptions 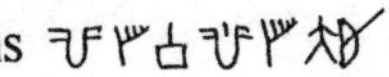 rau dha ṣu va dha ṣa (if understood correctly) says: if the sun is hot, the rain is in plenty. The experience of several years would have prompted them to make this remark. Therefore, whenever there would have been a hot summer, they would have prepared themselves for a heavy rainfall.

There are some small texts of two lines in which the first is always the same:  na ra, followed by  ra-ga,  va-ga and  ya-ga. It appears that the first is the observations of the nature and the others are the instructions following this. The clause na (river) ra (speed) seems to say: the river has begun flowing. Then there are three instructions: 1. ra (speed)-ga = Make haste! Perhaps it exhorts the people to utilize the flowing waters, so that not a drop of it goes waste. The clause na ra has itself later fossilised as nal (pipe) or nālā (canal). Certainly, the canals would have been dug out or artificial pipes were prepared by the potters to divert the waters to distant places. The second instruction va (dwelling)-ga advises to make reservoirs of waters or to store waters. Because va also means 'water', there may also be an instruction to irrigate the lands directly. The third instruction is not clear. Perhaps it advises to control the flow of water for specific purposes. Another form of the clause na ra (the river has begun flowing) is na da (flows and makes indistinct noise). It was fossilised as nada f. nadī (a big river). Here the flowing of rivers certainly relates to those coming from the Himalayas. It could be the instruction of the mid-summer after the snow had begun melting.

There is a text 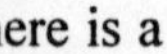 ḍha bu ṣa which perhaps means: the frogs predict or bring rains. They had observed that whenever the frogs croaked the rains followed.

Sometimes the whole weather situation is described in a lengthy statement: 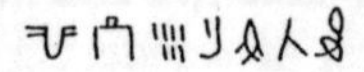 sa ma na nda ḍha bu ṣa = the summer has ended; the creatures are making noise; the frogs predict the rains. Generally, at the end of the summer, all the creatures cry for water. When there was the croaking of the frogs, they imagined that the rains were coming soon.

The modern meteorology hardly takes note of these creatures, although itself fails to make any correct forecast. The astronomical phenomena too are not taken into account in the modern weather forecast system. A stanza of the ancient astronomer Lalla says:

budha-śukrau samīpasthau sajalāṃ kuruto mahīm
tayor madhya-gato bhānuḥ samudram api śoṣayet.

"When Mercury and Venus are close to each other, the earth is flooded with water. If, however, the sun comes in the middle of them, even the ocean may dry up".

Because this stanza does not specify the area of rain-fall and drought, perhaps mentioned elsewhere, we can hardly make any use of it.

16

The Fire Discovered

The accented particle íd (only, alone), generally standing for the classical eva is, in its occurrences, almost restricted to the RV, though Prof. Thieme had seen jijīviṣa + id in jijīviṣec chataṃ samāḥ (Iśāvāsyop.1), and even céd (if) is analysed as ca + id and néd (least, never) as na + id. It is emphatic in the RV 1, 1, 4c (sa id deveṣu gachati) and more emphatic in 10, 168, 4 (ghoṣā id asya śṛṇvire na rūpam).

Phonetically corresponding to it, there is a small text  i dha in the Indus inscriptions, where the second syllable has just been deaspirated in passing from clause to a phrase and then to a lexeme. The Vedic meaning may help in understanding the Indus clause. If i is the primitive form of the pronoun i-d-am (it) and dha is for brightness, the clause simply means: it shines. If i is some noun, the clause may mean: this object (whatever it is) is very necessary for life. The clause turning into just a particle would have to travel through a tortuous path on an uneven land semantically. Also, it is difficult to determine the time consumed by this journey.

The object denoted by i in connection with dh may be fire, which later reflects in i (n) dh 'to kindle', édhas 'flame', etc. Then this idea leads us to the very beginning of the human culture, when the fire had just been discovered and its values had begun to be realised. At this stage of our understanding, we may surmise that the text means: the fire is useful or necessary (because it gives heat, cooks food, makes us warm in winter, terrifies the wild beasts, etc.).

Whatever the report furnished by the carbon-dating, it pushes our imagination several millenniums earlier.

The realization of the truth about the fire, its utterance as i dha and later its writing as  are the exercises of the span of time which we can just imagine but cannot determine. It should be left just here.

Just as there is i for 'fire', there would have been u for 'water' (later reflecting in udan 'water', etc.). The vocabulary of the primitive people would have been built just in this way.

17

Fire and Water

6115 

ca ṇa ra, ra ṇa bha

This text in two lines is not easily comprehensible, because the fossilised form of the two lines in Vedic too is not readily ascertainable.

If ca ṇa ra is theoretically reduced to *ca-n-rá, it requires the interposition of a -d- to become candrá 'shining'. It is not impossible. Because sū-nara (a good man) has emerged as su-nda-ra (beautiful) through *su-nnara (the long ū relieved by the double nn), we may have candrá through *can-rá from ca ṇa ra. On the basis of the meaning of candrá, we may suppose that ca (water) ṇa (creature) ra (speed) means: in the water the creatures move (= play). Often the reflection of the moon in the water would have been the point of reference. This may be the basis of candrá meaning 'shining'. That is to say, the fossilised form of the Indus clause ca ṇa ra may be the Vedic candrá 'shining', whatever the basis of the meaning.

Let us take the next clause ra ṇa bha. The Vedic nábh (RV 1, 174, 8) seems to be the fossilised form of ṇa bha, the later part of this clause. The syllable bha, extended by -va (= bhava-) means 'to be', by -ra (= bhara-) means 'to support', reduplicated bibhar- means 'to bear', and by -ya (= bhaya-) means 'to fear'. When it itself follows certain syllables, e.g. jabh 'to devour', 'destroy', dabh 'to injure', *gabh 'to be deep', dhabh (cf. the colloq. dhīp) 'to burn', it has, more or less, some injurious sense. Sāyaṇa takes nabh in the sense of hiṃsā (injury). But Geldner connects nábh with nábhas (cloud), and refers to similar other correspondences. Thus nábh for him is not different from nábhas.

But just as the Indus clause ṇa ga (the light has gone away) was reduced as nág (night) in Vedic, and there are many similar cases (ra ma : rám, ma ṣa : más, ma ṇa : mán, etc.), we may assume that nábh is the fossilised form of ṇa bha. Phonetically, there is not much decay, but in meaning the deviation is unimaginable.

Before its fossilization as nábh, ṇa bha would have been a clause of o + v type. Accordingly, it should have meant: a creature is injured. The first syllable ra in this line should be in the oblique case: through the fire a creature is injured. Then the Vedic nábh should just mean 'injury'. The RV 1, 174, 8 b perhaps means: for the removal of many serious injuries. If nábh is a concrete noun, it means 'an enemy': to ward off many formidable enemies.

The author of the Indus texts wants to distinguish fire and water through their action:

ca ṇa ra = in the water the creatures play.
ra ṇa bha = through the fire the creatures are injured.

Because the meanings jump like a frog, we cannot trace the stages of their development. But the phonetic development of a word does not leave us in uncertainty.

18

The Indus Weaponry

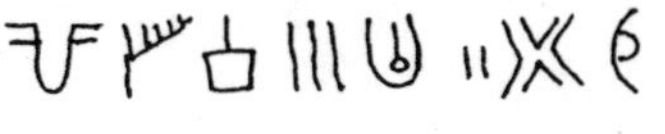

All the signs of the text, except the first from the right, are almost definitely identified. Because the second and third syllables yo ka reflect in a late Vedic vocable jyók 'for a long time', the first sign may be provisionally read ji. Thus the whole text reads as follows: ji yo ka gā va va dha ṣa.

The 4th and 5th syllables gā va, being in the middle of the text, is rather a lexical term (cattle) than a phrase (going into the stable) or a clause (goes into the stable).

The last syllable ṣa may be a verb, so that the preceding syllabic group va dha is a lexical word rather than a phrase or a clause. In the Vedic context, vadha means (1) killer, (2) a (deadly) weapon and (3) murder. If gāva (cattle) is the subject, vadha (a deadly weapon) may be the instrument made out of the horns of the cattle. Then gāva vadha ṣa perhaps means: the cattle provides weapons. The horns and hides of the cattle would have served such purposes.

The adverb jyók meaning 'for a long time' makes us conceive that ji (victory) yo (comfort) ka (time) may have converged on 'time-concept' after a tortuous journey: the whole text may now be interpreted thus: For a durable happiness the cattle provides weapons. The interpretation is not satisfactory in the form it has been put. Perhaps a more cogent idea is: For a long time the cattle have been providing us weapons through their horns and hides.

The meaning of the text suggests the very early state of the Indus society, when the milch cattle had begun to be domesticated and the parts of their body were variously utilized. They were still hunters, progressing towards agriculture.

19

The Snake Bites

pra da

This little text of two syllables can hardly be doubtful as to its reading. As regards the meaning, we are totally in dark. It could be a clause of the type s + v at the isolating stage of the Indus language. As a phrase also at the agglutinative stage, it could phonetically be the same. But at the inflexional stage, the accent falling on the last syllable, it could be reduced to *pṛdá.

In the AV, VS and TS, it occurs with its extended form pṛ́dāku (the accent thrown back on the first syllable), meaning 'a snake, viper, adder'. It occurs in the compound pṛ́dāku-sānu (snake-summited) in the RV (8, 17, 15). In the traditional lexicons, there are also other meanings: scorpion, tiger, elephant, tree.

These creatures are not harmless. Therefore, some injurious idea seems to lurk in *pṛdá. Whether it is a snake or scorpion or tiger or elephant, some of their organs or limbs appears to be the obvious factor on account of which these creatures are so called. Thus *pṛdá may be the sharp teeth of the snake, the pincer of the scorpion, the claw of the tiger and the trunk of the elephant. The Sanskrit root pīḍ 'to press, crush, torment' may be its later development.

The second syllable of the text, da, meaning 'pain' in the lexicons, is the first syllable in danta (tooth), from which ad 'to eat' developed in Vedic (through *ā-da 'past-eat', analysed as a-ad-a by the Vedic grammarians). Thus da of the text appears to be a verb meaning 'to bite, strike, injure'. Then pra is some 'injurious' creature, the sharp-toothed serpent itself (or the stinging scorpion or tiger or elephant).

A workable meaning of the text may be: (some specific) creatures (e.g. serpents) are injurious (to the human beings).

One may ask: what is the relevance of this text?

Here we are at the very beginning of the human civilisation. People were advised to be aware of the harmful creatures or animals. The heaths and natural landscapes were to be cleared off from the harmful creatures before founding villages or building houses.

Some archaeologist had once put the question: why these little messages were engraved on clay-tablets?

An objective answer may be this: Each message was to be carried to distant places, where it was to be disclosed and also explained to the people. That is why, there are many duplicates of the same message. It may be a part of their communication system throughout the empire. The clay-tablets are the primitive versions of the modern post-cards. The Indus texts mean much more than what is written algebrically:

pra da = the snake bites.
= the scorpion stings.
= the tiger pounces upon.
= the elephant crushes.

20

A Serpent-killer Invented

The idea of the existence of an advanced urban society in the Indus valley civilisation on the basis of the reports of excavations was somehow a handicap in understanding the language underneath the Indus script. When it has been discovered that the language represents the first or the isolating stage of the human speech typologically, it was natural to see or assume a primitive form of the society in it. The primitive type of the language in a primitive form of the society could reveal the natural and cogent meanings of the monosyllabic words of the grammar-less Indus language.

We will see the invention of the wheeled carts, mill-stones, siphoning instruments, etc. The Indian weapons are usually distinguished as as-tra (which is discharged, e.g. arrow, etc.) and śastra (which is held in hand, e.g. a sword, etc.). The following text perhaps relates to the invention of a weapon midway between an 'arrow' and a 'sword':

The text perhaps reads śa mu sa, though the central sign is still doubtful (see foot-note at the end). The meanings śa (weapon) mu (death :: to kill) sa (serpent) suggest that the clause is in the passive voice, the object (serpent) following the verb (to kill). The meaning of the text is : By a (specific) weapon the serpent is killed. The clause śa mu sa seems to have fossilised as śaṃs. In the countryside, a weapon to kill a crawling or creeping creature is called 'sahat' (a furrowed dart or lance), midway between 'arrow' and 'sword'. It is also phonetically different from śas-tra, that is, *śas-a-tra (the central -sa- becoming -ha-).

As they were gradually becoming aware of the dangers of the wild animals and harmful creatures like serpents, they had begun inventing various types of weapons; e.g. 'arrows' for shooting from a distance, 'swords' for killing from near, etc.

They also highlighted the importance of the object by means of the active and passive forms of the clause. If the importance of the object was to be emphasised, they used the passive form of the clause: the object put after the verb, the primitive way of the passive formation. Even in Sanskrit, the passive is an emphatic form of expression, on account of which the object is called ukta. Otherwise, in the active voice, it is anukta.

It is through the primitive type of language that we have come to know the primitive Indus society. When we have known the society, the dumb part of the language too is gradually becoming comprehensible to us.

The sign  has been assigned the value of mu. Among the vertically curved signs, only three are quotable: 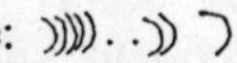 On the basis of the syllabic order of the Māheśvarasūtras, they stand, respectively, for : ña . . ṇa na. Though ṅ is rare even in Sanskrit, the absence of m is surprising. Because m is found with all vowels, its substitute was invented as above, having a number of variants for m- with different vowels.

21

The 'Cow' Domesticated

In order to correlate the importance of cow in the pastoral life of the Vedic people with the occurrence of bulls of various types as field-symbols and of the large number of sign-pair III in the Indus texts, it is reasonable to read this sign-pair as gā va. The gā value for the first sign is still a conjecture.

As a clause, gā va, being the verb gā 'to go' + the oblique case va 'dwelling', means 'goes into-the-dwelling (stable)'. But here gā va always occurs in the middle of the long texts. Therefore it is rather a lexical term (cattle, bull, cow) than a phrase or clause. This pastoral meaning of 'cow' was known to the Vedic tradition, which etymologises the Vedic go- 'cow' as gacchaṭi (i.e. a cow is so called because it goes). This brisk etymology does not show their acquaintance with va 'stable', which was both phonetically and semantically swallowed by the verb.

The isolating clause gā va (goes into the stable) contracted as phrase (going into the stable) or lexeme (cattle) gā-va at the agglutinative stage and had a plural form gāva-ṣa, but it was reduced to gāvas at the inflexional stage and analysed as gāv-as, laying the foundation of a new strong base gāu-. Pāṇini quotes Sphoṭāyana who knew a base gava-, and gāvī, a feminine form from gāva-, was also known to Patañjali. Thus at least two terms for 'cow', gauḥ at the higher level of speech and gāva at the lower level, were current in the Vedic society. The social hierarchy reflected in the language. The higher class of the society spoke the inflexional Vedic and the lower level spoke the agglutinative Indus, on account of which some rustic and outlawed groups of them were called mṛdhra-vāk (rudely speaking) and kṛṣṇa-tvak (black-skinned).

It appears that gāva stood for the milch-cattle in general, which was later restricted to the bovine class. The sign-pair gā va appears 126 times in the long texts, and it is certainly a lexical term (cattle) there. A few small texts may be shown here.

While reporting on the excavations on the Indus basin in Pakistan (National Geographic, Vol. 197, No. 6, June 2000, p. 118), Mike Edwards seems to agree with a farmer: ... "The Zebu is far smarter than the water buffalo, which is also used for farmwork. Zebus are geniuses." This view agrees with the following Indus text if understood correctly: 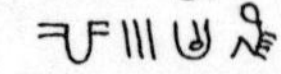 dhā (white) gāva (bull) ṣa (wise) seems to say: The white bulls know (what to do). Colloquially, a bull is called dhākar, which perhaps reflects in the sign-pair  dhā gra. In a different context, there is an often-quoted remark: goṣu kṛṣṇā bahu-kṣīrā (among the cows the black one gives plenty of milk). The following text seems to say something like this: 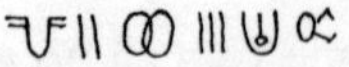 bha (shining) gāva (cow) cha (milk) ra (speed) ṣa (nipple) = Plenty of milk flows from the nipple of the black cows. Perhaps ra ṣa (flows from the nipple) had turned up as the bisyllabic verb. The text simply says: Plenty of milk flows from the black cow.

The following text perhaps warns about the particular variety of the cattle:  ni (blue) gāva (cattle) śa (injury) ṣa (embryo) = The blue cattle causes injury. Perhaps it refers to the untamed blue variety, having sharp horns, which are generally dangerous.

A different statement is made about the same animal in the following text: 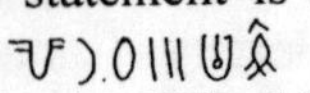 ni (blue) gāva (cattle) ca (oyster) na (pearl) ṣa (embryo) = The blue cattle are pearls in the oyster. In spite of its harmful character, it was a good rare breed and sought after.

A text 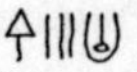 gā va ṣa is either the plural form of the lexeme gāva- (cow) or a clause meaning 'the cows are there'. Perhaps the office in charge of the milch-cattle used to keep such seals.

All these texts points to the state of the Indus society which was just coming to farming and was gradually giving up hunting.

22

Domestication of Horses

Of all the syllables in Sanskrit, ha has the largest number of meanings in the lexicons of the monosyllabic words. In the Māheśvarasūtras ha has been enumerated twice: one at the beginning of the consonants and the other at their end. From its positioning in the Māheśvarasūtras, one ha at the beginning of the voiced consonants and the other ha at the end of the voiceless consonants, prompt us to believe that the first ha is voiced and the last ha is voiceless. But the RV-Prātiśākhya 14, 28 regards the voicelessness in h as a fault in pronunciation. However, this also suggests that the voiced and voiceless h were known to the phoneticians of the RV-Prātiśākhya. Even Bodding points out that there are both voiced and voiceless h in Santhali, the latter either lost at the initial position in some dialects or represented by k finally in some other dialects. The Sanskrit grammarians explain the two h of the Māheśvarasūtras as forming two types of Pratyāhāras, the one with the initial h (ha-ś) and the other with the final h (śa-l). The final h turns into k in Sandhi conditions in Sanskrit (lih : a-lik-ṣa-t), which reveals its voiceless nature in its prehistory. In Indus there were certainly voiceless and voiced h and, because the syllabic order of the Māheśvarasūtras is just a slightly edited copy of the Indus syllabary, two h were retained by the Sanskrit school.

Of the several meanings of ha, one is 'horse'. Elsewhere, we have seen that h̲a- has been variously extended in the later languages: h̲a (Indus), h̲a-śva > áśva, h̲a-rva > arvā (Vedic), h̲a-śpha > aspa (Avesta), h̲a-kva > equus (Latin), h̲a-pva > hippos (Gk.) h̲a-r-sa > hors (Germanic).

In the following two texts, ha means 'horse': 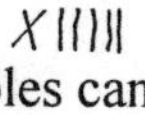 ha (horse) ya (active) = the horses are active. Later, the syllables came together and haya was a phrase (the active or nimble horse). In Sanskrit, this haya is said to have been derived from hi 'to send'.

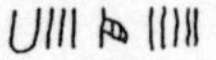 ha (horse) ra (speed), va (dwelling) ga (inj.) = the horses run away; keep them in the stable.

It was perhaps the time when the wild horses had begun to be domesticated in the Indus society. As we go on reading the Indus texts, we find ourselves at the primitive state of the Indus civilisation. Naturally, the isolating stage of the language should not lead us beyond it. On the other hand, the ruins of the cities indicate a very advanced civilisation, which do not find mention in the texts.

We have been now able to discover reasons for the absence of such texts. As the civilisation advanced, the Indus language too gradually reached the next, that is, the agglutinative stage. But for the agglutinative type of language, the clay-tablets were no more useful. There were polysyllabic words and longer clauses in short or big paragraphs. Perhaps they began to write on some spacious materials like palm-leaves, bark of the birch-trees, etc. The documents inscribed on such perishable materials could not survive when the civilisation collapsed due to some natural disaster.

The later phase of the language documented in the metrical Vedic literature could come down to us, because it was śruti.

23

The Hoof of a Horse is Dangerous

This unique text with three animal signs only (from right to left), 1. a hare (śaśa for *śa-sa 'long-eared' cf. Latin caso), 2. the hood of a serpent (phaṭa, phaṇa) and 3. a bat (jatu), each being the first syllable of some Sanskrit word, is probably one of the oldest of the inscriptions, when the geometrical and numeral signs had not come in common use. It shows that the Indus people had begun domesticating the useful wild animals. We have to interpret this text with this background.

If the identification of the signs is correct, the text seems to read: śa pha ja. The first two syllables make an old vocable śapha 'hoof of a horse' (Av. safa), the syllable-wise analysis of which, through the traditional Sanskrit lexicons of the monosyllabic words, confirms this meaning: The syllable śa being the first element of śas (to kill) and its derivatives (śastra 'weapon', etc.) stands for some 'injurious instrument'; pha stands for 'abcess', and ja for the ideas associated with 'birth', e.g. to cause'. Then the text seems to say: some injurious instrument causes abcess. Because śa (injurious instrument) + pha (abcess) makes śapha (hoof), the 'injurious instrument' is the 'hoof' itself and śa itself means 'hoof'. The verb ja (causes) has become irrelevant after the formation of the word śapha.

The analysis or etymology of the word śapha in the manner of a prehistoric language makes us think about the activities of these primitive people. They were still engaged in hunting and domesticating useful wild animals, specially horses, and were careful not to be hit by their hindlegs. They had learnt many things through their previous errors.

The Vedic people used this śapha in various contexts. In śaphā-ruj 'inflicting by śapha', the inflicting agent is sometimes an animal, sometimes a magician. In relation to a magician, śapha was associated with śāpa 'curse' and later a verb śap 'to inflict by curse, to abuse' was deduced from śapha, because the loss of aspiration was thought to be compensated by the long vowel in śāpa. This śāpa: śapha relationship (the length in vowel being identical with the aspiration in a consonant) is now explained through the laryngeal H.

SAD 'to ride on the horse-back'

1. h̲a da 
2. h̲a da ṣa 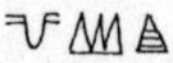
3. h̲a da ṣa gha 
4. h̲a da ṣa gha 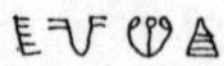
5. h̲a da ṣa gha 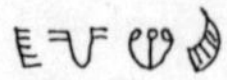

This group of texts is basically the extension of the first text h̲a da, initially with ṣa, then with the future-affix gha. In the 4th and 5th texts, the second sign is the geometrical version of da, and in the 5th text the first sign is the animal version of h̲a.

Of the several meanings of h̲a, the 'horse' is very relevant with reference to the early phase of the Indus valley civilisation. Then this dangerous but useful animal had begun to be domesticated. The hindleg of the horse  is a sign for la (reflecting in the colloquial lathār 'strike by the hindleg').

In the two-sign text h̲a da, da is a verb. It means 'pain' as well as 'mountain'. With its verbal sense, it may indicate 'riding' which could be painful or dangerous. Then h̲a da seems to mean: the horse is painful or dangerous to ride. It was a stage of the civilisation when the wild horse had begun to be domesticated and there were many painful experiences with this animal. By the time the clause h̲a da had been reduced phonetically to <u>sad</u>, during which the isolating Indus reached the inflexional stage, the horse was already domesticated and trained to carry men and material to distant places. Then <u>sad</u> meant 'to sit on the horse-back' But the memory of the painful experiences was also attached with this sad: to sink down, be in distress, perish, specially when preceded by certain prepositions.

The English 'saddle', coming through the Germanic sources, also indicates its original connection with the 'horse-back'. Even in Sanskrit, a horse-rider is called aśva-sādin, though sad was long ago attached with 'sitting' in the sacrificial sessions, from which sat-tra 'sacrificial session' was derived, which had no memory of its relation with the horse-back.

When ẖa da was extended with ṣa, da was no more a verb. It was a noun, having the same meaning as it later had in da-ma (house), literally (da 'pain' -ma 'end') meaning 'end of misery', because it provided comfort and prosperity (cf. RV 1, 1, 8 : vardhamānaṃ sve dame 'prospering in own house'). As da has also 'mountain' as its meaning, the horse-back was also suggestive of some 'high seat'.

Then ẖa da ṣa seems to say: the horse provides a high seat. In the process of the domestication of the horses, people used to ride on it. Though not quite comfortable, it was after all a high seat, a moving home. Therefore, the phonetically reduced form sádas means 'seat, place, assembly'. Geldner rightly means 'saddle' by sádas in the RV 5, 61, 2. Thus sad- of sádas is not different from the same of saddle (Anglo-Saxon sadul).

The same text extended by gha is just the expression of 'futurity' or even 'emphasis': ẖa da ṣa gha = the horse will serve as abode (in carrying men and material from one place to another).

The usefulness of the horse had been realised to its full extent. These little texts narrate the full history of the domestication of horses.

Needless to say, we have no doubt about the existence of horses in the Indus civilisation. The archaeology has already proved it, and the Indus language proves it more emphatically.

24

Founding a Village

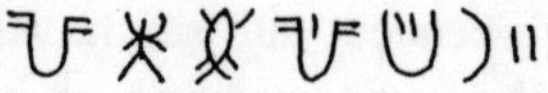

If the text is correctly read, the first part seems to terminate at the fourth syllable, suggested by the verb ṣa bent towards ṣu. The two clauses, ta na gi ṣu and ha gra ṣa, appear to be syntactically connected through some conjunction, probably through "because", resulting in some drastic step.

Now we know the state of the Indus society better than earlier. At the time of the writing of the inscriptions, it had just crossed the border of hunting and gathering and was stationed on the early stage of farming. The people had begun eating coarse flour, as we have met with the clause form of the Vedic vocable dṛṣád (mill-stone) in the extant Indus texts. The wheeled carts had been invented. Though a watchman had begun to be employed and dogs had begun to be domesticated to guard the property, suggesting the process of abandoning the nomadic life, there is no mention of the founding of a village.

If grā-ma is an agglutinative formation, -ma shows the cessation of wandering concealed in ga (movement) and ra (speed) of gra. If -ma is a past-affix (as in rā-ma 'fire-past' > 'burnt' > 'a black one'), grā-ma is a phrase meaning 'cessation of wandering' from the clause 'the wandering stopped'. It was the beginning of the concentration of the community in one locality.

That is to say, we have to interpret this text with a mind hardly stretching beyond the agricultural society before the founding of villages. We have seen the first part of grāma (village) in this text.

One of the lexical meanings of ta is a 'thief' or a 'wicked man', and the same of na is 'jewel', which may suggest the movable property in general. Then the following giṣa- appears to be a bisyllabic verb. It reflects in geṣ- 'to search' of the Dhātupāṭha. In the context of the meanings of ta and na, giṣa- may be supposed to mean 'to take away, rob'. A possible meaning of the first clause may be: By the thief the jewel is stolen, or, by the robbers the property is taken away.

Of the several meanings of ha, sa-kopa-vāraṇa (preventing angrily) reflects in the colloquial ha addressed to a draught animal to make it stop. The following gra (wandering) ṣa (end) repeats the same advice. Thus ha gra ṣa means : stop ! make an end to wandering.

Now we arrive at a cogent meaning of the text: Because the robbers take away the property, stop (and) make an end to the nomadic life.

This decision was drastic. It was the beginning of concentrating at one place and founding a village.

We are gradually realising that the Indus society is still continuing in the remote countryside of India. We also realise that the traditional Sanskrit lexicons of the monosyllabic words are quite reliable, although Roth was suspicious and ironical about it.

25

The Perils of the Village Life

If this text reads cō ra, ra-ga, we are at the very beginning of the village life in the Indus valley civilisation. In its ordinary form, the quadrangular or rhomboid sign, graphically varying with the oval sign, reads ca. But cō value has been given to this decorated sign on the basis of cora (thief) of the late Sanskrit. Perhaps co itself means 'thief' at the isolating stage of Indus, and ra (speed) signifies 'running away'; therefore, cora literally means: the thief is running away, later becoming the phrase 'the running thief' and then the lexeme 'thief'. The following ra-ga simply means: run (after him)!

If the meaning is correct (and there is hardly any doubt about it), we are at the very early phase of the Indus valley civilisation. Perhaps 'villages' (grāma = g-rā-ma 'cessation of wandering) had begun to be established and the nomadic life of hunting and food-gathering had been given up. At this stage, the less privileged or poor people of the society or of the neighbouring village had become addicted to theft and robbery.

The text appears to be the 'alarm-word', just as even now in the countryside the village-chowkidārs raise the voice 'be awake'. In the colloquial dialects, even now, we hear the verb raged-. It is perhaps a part of some prehistoric clause, because a doubtful text elsewhere, that is, 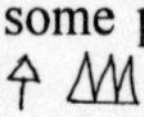 reads: da ṣa, which perhaps means: in the mountains (da) they dwell (ṣa). If it follows the preceding ra-ga in a different context, it means: chase away the mountain-dwellers. Now, raged- means 'to chase away'. The clause or the phrase da ṣa seems to be the precursor of the Vedic Dāsa (and Dasyu), the outlawed group of the Vedic society, who used to indulge in theft and robbery.

Because the ethnology of ancient India had been badly distorted by the philological researches of the late 19th and early 20th centuries, these Dāsas and Dasyus were conceived as 'evil beings' and 'enemies of gods'. Some individual ones of them were named particularly, namely: Śambara, Śuṣṇa, Cumuri, Dhuni, variously called ayajña, ayajyu, anās, etc. If Cumuri was one of them, the centre of an Indus text  va cu mu rau ṇa ci śa seems to read this name in some primitive form. It is not possible to comprehend this text now, but the individual syllables faintly suggest these thieves and theft.

As we gradually go on reading the text, we realise that every good and bad aspect of the Vedic culture reflects in the ruins of the Indus valley civilisation and its inscriptions.

26

The 'rags' of the Rustic Dialects

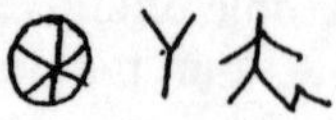

If we read this text from right to left, it is : ri ḍha ci/ce; if we read it from left to right, it is : ci/ce ḍha ri. If ḍha is dentalised and devoiced, the left-to-right reading gives a colloquial word ce/cithrī 'rags'. From the right-to-left reading, no identifiable word comes out. In Santhali and some other Bihari dialects, there is cethrā/cithrī 'rag, tatter, worn out piece of cloth', the latter exactly corresponding to the Indus text read from left to right. Provisionally, we accept the left-to-right reading.

Individually, the syllables ci/ce (ce = thief), ḍha (dog) ri (ra = speed , fire) bring us to a situation like this: In the primitive Indus villages, the thief would come at night. The dogs would run after him, overtake him and snatch the cloths worn by the thief. The tattered cloths worn by the thief would have been given back to the master. Then ci/ce ḍha ri appears to mean: from the thief the dog takes away (the cloths). In Hindi proverbs, we hear something like this : even if rags are recovered from the fleeing ghost, it is alright.

It is true, these meanings are purely speculative, but they do not go beyond the possible state of affairs. Moreover, some words of the colloquial languages are not derivable from the Sanskrit sources but are traceable in the Santhal dictionary. Some similar texts, e.g. 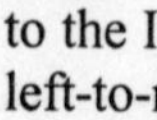 dhī ṭha 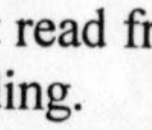 dhī ṣṭha appear to reflect in the Santhal dictionary. Cf. ḍhīṭ(h) 'obstinate'.

The researches on the Indian languages have been very superficial, and the results have been generally hasty and presumptuous. Thus the language of the Aśokan inscriptions has been said to be the old Prakrit. Though Santhali is morphologically the same as Bhojpuri, Maithili and other Bihari dialects, it is said to belong to the Austric family.

It is meant to say that the fossilised forms of the Indus texts are traceable not only in the socalled Aryan languages but also in the Munda and Dravidian groups of languages.

27

The Watchman

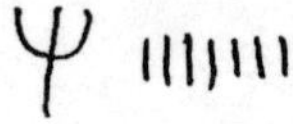

This two-sign small text in two lines reads well: ṭha ṇa. But, nevertheless, it is not easily comprehensible.

Standing alone, a syllable is most likely to be a verb: ṭha (disc or circle) = to go round, ṇa (knowledge) = to know. An isolated verb is most likely to express an order and, because the usual injunctive affix ga is not attached to it, the language is typically at the isolating stage. If ṭha means 'go round' and ṇa means 'know', we may find ourselves near some constabulary in the suburbs of an Indus city.

Even now a rustic term ṭhullā is used for a constable, which may be the corrupt form of the phrase *ṭhaṇa (one who goes round and enquires about), because l has generally resulted from some original n through r (cf. śarvan+ī = śarvar-ī 'night'). Then this text exhorts the agent working as a watchman to go round the area and know the state of affairs, because the society had just crossed the line of the primitive tribal stage and was now running under a civil administration. A sense of security had developed among them and they were apprehensive of the rogue elements of the society.

The ruins of the Indus valley civilisation portray an advanced state of the society, but their language speaks of a primitive culture. There is no incongruity about it, because the culture advances more rapidly than the language. Even now, a mobile phone has virtually demolished the telephone exchanges but the language is exactly the same as when a telephone apparatus was reported to be 'speaking' in a human voice.

28

A Dog as a Guard

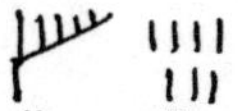

ḍha dha

This little text occurs more than once. One of the meanings of ḍha in the traditional Sanskrit dictionaries of the monosyllabic words is a 'dog', which itself represents the sound ḍha among the animal figures. Obviously, it is a clause. The first syllable may be either the subject or the object, the second being the verb. In the first case, the clause may be supposed to mean: the dog guards (the property). In the second case, it may mean: let the dog guard (the property). Also: the dog barks (to ward off thieves).

The fossilised form of the clause may be seen in the rustic and colloquial expression 'dhat' = be off. It is generally used to drive out somebody or some animal. In the expression 'dhat tere kī', it borders on abuse in a mild tone. It is here a noun, meaning 'expulsion'.

We cannot say anything more, but let us consider the circumstances under which it would have been written. Because the dog is involved, the situation borders on 'hunting'. It may also be already within the boundary of the civilized life under civil administration, the domesticated dog employed to guard the property.

Even the modern pastoral society employs the trained dogs to guard the herds of sheep.

At the agglutinative stage of Indus, this clause itself would have turned up as a bisyllabic verb meaning 'to go away', which still now reflects in dhat. It could not transit into the inflexional Vedic, but dhik 'fie upon' from dhigh = dhagh may be its proto-type.

29

The Wheeled Carts Invented

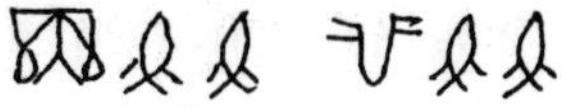

na na ṭha   na na ṣa

The reading of the two texts is doubtless. The fossilised form of the first may be nart (nṛt) 'to dance' through *nant from *nánat, on the analogy of va ṇa ṭha > *vánat > *vant > vart (vṛt) 'to turn round, revolve'. But corresponding to vanád (fire) from the same va ṇa ṭha, there is no *nanád from na na ṭha. The meaning of nṛt gives some clue about the meaning of the Indus clause na na ṭha. The verb ṭha (disc, circle) meaning 'to turn round, revolve' suggests that na is something like wheel, the dual na na referring to the "two wheels of a cart". The meaning of the clause may be: the two wheels of the cart turn round the axle.

Unless two wheels are fixed on the two ends of the axle, the cart cannot go. The emphasis of the text appears to lie on the "two wheels". Though the wheel had been invented, e.g. in respect of pottery, etc., for a cart two wheels were required. Some draught animal, either alone or in pair, was yoked from the front, as we have two wheeled bullock-carts even today in the countryside. We suppose that every item of the primitive Indus society is continuing in India, at least in the countryside.

A later form, certainly at the agglutinative stage, seems to be ratha 'chariot' from ra (speed) + tha (wheel). Burrow's etymology of ratha is more ingenious than correct.

If na na with ṭha are 'the two wheels' of a cart, let us examine what the same can be with ṣa. The clause na na ṣa too should have fossilised as *nanas > *nans > *narṣ (nṛṣ) on the analogy of ta na ṣa (from the womb gems come out) > tánas (offspring RV. 5, 70, 4) > *tans > tarṣ (tṛṣ) 'to be thirsty'. Unfortunately, there is no *narṣ (nṛṣ) in the Vedic vocabulary.

However, there is nṛṣāḥ (RV 9, 2, 10). But go-ṣāḥ, aśva-sāḥ and vāja-sāḥ in the same stanza force us to analyse nṛṣā as nṛ + sā from san 'to procure'. Though go-ṣā 'giving cows', aśva-sā 'giving horses' and vāja-sā 'giving food' have cogent meanings, nṛṣā meaning 'giving men' is not exactly or correctly so. Even yoṣā 'woman', doṣā 'darkness' and joṣa- in joṣam (silently) have no identifiable vocable as the first member. On the other hand, yoṣā may be traced in the Indus inscriptions as yo ṣa  (gives pleasure).

We wonder, why nṛṣāḥ cannot be analysed as nṛṣ-ás like tṛṣ-ā from tṛṣ 'thirst', mṛṣ-ā (falsely) from *mṛṣ, vṛṣ-án from vṛṣ, as also like yoṣ-an, doṣ-ā and joṣ-a ! The Vedic language is so young in comparison with the various stages of Indus that the real or original meaning jumps like a frog in unpredictable ways.

If na na are the 'two wheels' even in the clause na na ṣa, something intimately connected with the 'two wheels' is referred to and the 'action' indicated by it is meant by the verb ṣa. The text perhaps gives instruction on the making of the wheeled carts. The two nails on the two sides of the axle is referred to which stops the wheels from slipping out. Then the text exactly means; two wheels are stopped (by the nails from slipping out); alternatively: (the nails) stop the two wheels (from slipping out).

The word nṛṣāḥ < nṛṣ-ás of the RV may literally be 'stopper': one who averts evils, injury or misery.

30

The Flour-mill Invented

1410 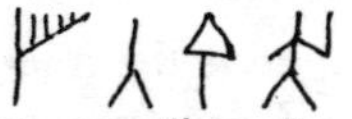

dra ṣa ṭha dha

The reading of the text appears to be doubtless, as far as possible. Without going to the meaning of the text, we may theoretically try to trace its phonetic development in the later phase of the language.

If the accent falls on the second syllable ṣa, the first syllable dra may possibly be reduced to dṛ, and the third syllable ṭha may possibly be transformed into d (on the analogy of va ṇa ṭha becoming vanád, otherwise becoming *vánat > vant > vart/vṛt). If, just theoretically, dra ṣa ṭha may transform into dṛṣád, there is actually a word dṛṣád in the Vedic vocabulary, meaning 'stone', specifically the 'lower one of the two mill-stones', coming down to the last record of the classical Sanskrit.

This meaning of dṛṣád may perhaps help to reveal the meaning of the Indus clause dra ṣa ṭha. (Let us, for the time being, forget the following dha.) The syllable da meaning 'mountain' agrees with 'stone' for the whole dṛṣád, and the following ra (speed) justifies the prefixed 'mill-' in 'mill-stone'. Thus dra is perhaps the 'moving, grinding stone', the upper one of the two grinding stones. The final ṭha (circle, disc) may be the verb, meaning 'to turn round'. Thus the subject dra and the verb ṭha mean: the (grinding) stone turns round. The meanings of ṣa quotable from the traditional lexicons do not help. Therefore, following the context, we may take it to mean 'the lower stone': dra ṣa ṭha = the (upper) grind-stone turns round the (static) lower stone. How the lower part of the two mill-stones began to dominate the meaning could not have been predicted. Otherwise, ṣa may also refer to the post round which the mill-stone turns: the mill-stone turns round the post. More cogently it may be translated also thus: the upper mill-stone turns round the lower mill-stone (and) crushes (the corn).

Perhaps the last syllable too is a verb. We have associated dha elsewhere with 'light' (to shine, to be hot, etc.), but the most appropriate meaning here appears to be 'to crush, powder'. Perhaps we have arrived at a workable meaning: the (upper) grind-stone turns round the (static lower) stone/post (and) crushes (the corn).

Now we should examine the relevance of the text. It appears to be a text of the Indus community when it was just at the beginning of urbanization. The mill-stones had been invented to grind corns for consumption, and the system had to be popularized through mass communication. It indicates a stage when people had begun eating the crushed or powdered version of the corn. Before it they used to consume the whole corn.

Now, the text appears to say: the upper mill-stone turns round the lower mill-stone (post) and crushes the corn in the form of flour. We see how the Indus society was proceeding towards urbanization. The society was as much in the infancy of urbanization as the language itself was in its childhood, just at the isolating stage.

Some scholar in a private communication had expressed surprise at my visualizing a language with monosyllabic words and no grammar in respect of homo sapiens who could have attained a high degree of sophistication in urbanization with excellent town-planning, etc. As a matter of fact, we should not gauge the material advancement with the linguistic development, because the former runs like a tiger and the latter moves like a turtle.

Moreover, the ruins of the Indus culture should not synchronies with the isolating stage of the language. Unfortunately, the records of the agglutinative stage, perhaps written on perishable materials, several centuries later, should have been lost.

31

Fodder for the Domesticated Cattle

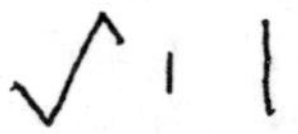

la pa ma

(Time Plant Death)

In course of time the plants perish

This text had been discussed in “The RV in the Indus Inscriptions” p. 101 (2003). While the meaning proposed there is hardly doubtful, the context in which this text appears has to be found out. It is true that the isolating clauses mean much more than what is briefly stated.

The meaning ‘komalaṃ tṛṇam’ (the tender grass) recorded in the traditional Sanskrit lexicons for the Vedic fossil úlupa of this clause of the isolating stage is suggestive of its usefulness for the domesticated cattle of the early Indus civilisation. Perhaps the horses and cows had already been domesticated for which the fodder was required regularly. Because the buffalo was still a mṛga (wild animal) in the RV (9, 96, 6), it could not have been domesticated so early.

Though the plants for fodder could have been cultivated for the domesticated animals, this text perhaps speaks of the grasses growing wild or uncultivated, as in most cases even now. The people were advised to harvest the uncultivated grasses before they perished seasonally according to their short span of life. Because the grasses were tender, they were fit for the animals. Even the peasants found them easy to harvest.

We suppose that these little texts on clay-tablets were widely circulated among the peasants, who had already settled at different places, founding villages and building houses for themselves. It was the stage of the civilisation when the nomadic life had been given up for ever.

We think that there were separate dwellings for the domesticated animals. At the isolating stage of the language, va was the 'dwelling' in general. Later, cattle were mentioned as 'going into the dwelling' (gā-va), the term later referring only to the bovine cattle. At the Vedic stage, when the sense of dwelling was completely lost in gāva (cattle, f. gāvī), it was further extended as gavasthāna (a place for the cattle), which continues till today as bathān.

The human dwelling was later, at the agglutinative stage of the language, da-ma (cessation of pain), having the sense of comfort. It is of the same formation as grā-ma (cessation of wandering).

Now the context in which the text la pa ma was circulated is quite clear. The villagers were advised to make the best use of the seasonal crops meant for the animals. Even now the villagers know when what to do.

32

The Man Builds His House

va ṇa ra

The reading of the text is doubtless. In the early Vedic language, the clause va ṇa ra has fossilised as vánar, which is attested through the compounds vanar-gú and -ṣád of somewhat controversial meaning. The real meaning of vánar- has been obscured by its supposed identity with vánas = vana, in spite of the evident phonetic difficulty, namely the appearance of r in place of s, suggested by Sāyaṇa.

The word vanar-gú relates to fire (RV 1, 145, 5) and to robber (RV 10, 4, 6. AV 4, 36, 7), and the word vanar-ṣád relates to bird (RV 2, 31, 1) and fire (RV 10, 46, 7). While the fire and the bird can be easily associated with 'wood', the robber has hardly anything to do with it. In AV 4, 36, 7 vanar-gú is distinguished from stena, which semantically oppose each other as 'insider' and 'outsider'.

By the use of -gu and -sad as the second member, it is clear that vanar- is some destination in the first case and seat in the second which could be altar for the fire, nest for the bird and den for the robber. The exact meaning of vanar-, however, has not come out.

If we interpret the clause va (dwelling) ṇa (animal) ra (speed), it seems to give the meaning: in the dwelling the animals go. Perhaps the first element 'dwelling' dominates the whole clause when it was fossilised as the lexeme vanar-. That is to say, vanar means 'dwelling' in the broad sense of the term.

Perhaps the clause va ṇa ra refers to a time when the Indus people had started making dwellings for themselves. They had left the caves long ago and had started wandering in search of food. Their concentration at one place after giving up wandering was the founding of 'villages', which literally means 'the end of wandering' (grā 'wandering' + ma 'end'). At this stage, they required a *vánar for themselves. It was the early stage in the cultural life of the Indus people. Specifically, vanar-gú was perhaps the newcomer in the house, like the fire of the kitchen or the robber, while vanar-sád was the permanent resident, like the bird of the nest or the fire of the altar.

33

The Beginning of Pottery

dhī rau dha

The last two syllables from the right, that is, rau dha, reflect in a colloquial word raüdā 'the hot sun, the heat of the sun'. At its clause stage, it could have meant: the sun is hot. Then the first syllable from the right is a noun in some oblique case: in the day the sun is very hot.

As regards the reading of the first sign, it is probably dhī, which reflects in di-na, div 'day', dīdivi 'shining', dīdhiti 'light'. If the four strokes or the ribs of the backbone stands for e, it may also be dhe. In fact, there are nine variants of the ribbed sign, and not only the shape but also the number of ribs vary from three to five. Thus we may assume that all the variants stand for dh- with different vowels. It has often been suggested that all the variants should have been appropriately indicated and the normalization of signs should have been avoided.

We may also opine on the context of this inscription. The message 'during the day the sun is hot' perhaps leads us to pottery. The earthen pots were manufactured during the night and exposed to the sun-light during the day. Perhaps it was the very beginning of the earthen potteries. The purport of the inscription is much more than what it actually states. The people were advised to work at night and take rest during the day while the manufactured pots were being dried up in the sunlight.

This text had become readable as early as 1997 (From Indus to Sanskrit, Pt. III, p. 104), but its meaning has surfaced now when we have been able to know the state of culture of the Indus people. If 3500 BC is the beginning of the Indus valley civilisation, this inscription belongs to the neighbourhood of this epoch.

34

A Happy Home

ẖa ma ha

There is no doubt about the reading of the text which is from left to right in this case. It is just so, because it is the only instance of the voiceless ẖ being at the extreme left. Otherwise, it is mainly at the beginning and, sometimes, in the middle from the right. Therefore, the left-to-right reading is preferable here.

The initial ẖ is lost in Vedic, as, for example, in ẖa-ṣ-ṭa > aṣṭa = 8, ẖa-ś-va > aśva = the injuriously strong horse, etc. The last ha lost its vowel due to accent on the preceding syllable and, later, the Indus clause ẖa ma ha emerged as amā́ in Vedic, originally a noun meaning 'home' but later always an adverb 'at home, nearby'. The unquotable nominal sense indicates that the word originated long before the beginning of the Ṛgvedic hymns.

The initial h seems to have been retained in Germanic: Anglo-Saxon hām, Eng. home, Germ. Heim, Gothic Heims. Even in 'horse' the original h has been retained in Germanic, while it was lost in all other dialects except Greek.

Now we may come to the interpretation of the Indus text. Because the voiceless and voiced h became indistinguishable in Vedic, only ha comprises all the meanings in the Ekākṣara-koṣas. The voiceless ẖa perhaps means 'home' itself, the meaning having been retained in all the dialects even when the clause was fossilised as a lexical term. The central ma means 'happiness', and the last ha is the verb meaning 'to cause'. Thus the clause ẖa ma ha means:

the home gives happiness. As a phrase, it would have meant 'a happy home'.

From its earliest occurrences, amā́ is an adverb in Vedic: 'at home, near at hand, nearby', later 'together'. There is a compound amā-júr 'growing old at home (in father's house) and a derivative amā-tya 'house-companion, minister'. The word itself hardly survived in the later phase of the language. The word amāvasyā has amā- as the first member, but literally the word is not very clear.

Though the etymological dictionaries derive every Vedic word from the Vedic material, we see how the Vedic language is rooted deeper in the ruins of Indus. Even the words of the socalled IE dialects are rooted in the ur-Sanskrit. But nothing goes beyond it, because it is the first human speech.

The socalled IE communities disintegrated from Indus as fully civilized and urbanized people. They were no more nomads. Only the limited space accompanied by some tragic events obliged them to go to Central Asia and then to Europe. Wherever they went, they founded villages and built houses. Only when the space became congested, they migrated forward.

35

The Oil-lamp

h̲a ci ra

The reading of the text is certainly doubtless, but before ascertaining its meaning let us analyse it phonetically.

If the initial h̲a is reduced to a-, and the central syllable ci, having the affricate value (tśi), is reduced to śi, we have a fossilised vocable aśira meaning 'sun, fire, diamond' in the traditional Sanskrit lexicons. That is to say, some shining object is referred to by it, which may be sought in the individual syllables of the text.

The final ra itself means 'fire', and it may have the status of a verb (= burns). Then ci may be its subject, meaning perhaps a 'lamp' (reflecting through cit 'knowledge' = a form of light). The breathing h̲ at the first syllable probably means 'oil' (through its inherent overtone) in the oblique case. The text thus seems to means: through the oil a lamp burns (and there is light inside the house).

It is obviously a laboured and fabricated meaning. As we search for its relevance, we may suppose that after these people had founded villages by giving up the nomadic life and built houses for their comfort, they required the houses to be lighted. They would have discovered that the oil exuded from specific corn produces light through the fire. Even in the Sanskrit drama Sākuntala of Kālidāsa we learn that the ascetics used the stones to crush the iṅgudī-fruits to exude oil from them (iṅgudī-phalabhida upalāḥ). Even though there would have been oil-mills in the cities, the ascetics used the means available to them in the forest. In the countryside, the villagers even now continue the traditions of the primitive society, though they were given up long ago in the urban life.

It must be accepted that ẖa meaning 'oil' is a daring attempt at the interpretation, because it has no clue for this meaning, except the doubtful context itself.

It is now clear that the isolating stage of the Indus language gives the picture of a primitive society advancing very rapidly towards civilisation.

Although it is difficult to date an event, this language depicts the society of a neo-lithic age when hunting and gathering had stopped and the farming had started with crude non-metallic implements.

36

The Cattle-breeding

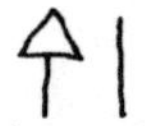

la ṣa

The reading of this bisyllabic text in two lines in doubtless. To arrive at its cogent meaning, we may first analyse it phonetically.

The Indus clause would have become a phrase and then a lexeme laṣa. The first syllable la may have undergone rhotacism. If the accent falls on the second syllable at the inflexional stage, *raṣa may have become *ṛṣá. It was extended to ṛṣa-bhá 'bull'. From *ṛṣá a verb ṛṣ 'to flow' seems to have been deduced. Later, even vṛṣ 'to spray' developed from ṛṣ, and it had a derivative vṛ́ṣ-an, extended to vṛṣa-bhá.

It is doubtless that the clause la ṣa has ultimately fossilised as vṛṣ-, giving birth to vṛ́ṣ-an 'bull' in the later phase of the language.

In the early phase of the Indus civilisation, when cows and horses had begun to be domesticated, they would have thought of multiplying the number of these useful animals. It is perhaps in this context that they would have conceived a clause with a suggestive meaning. There is some sort of equation between the original Indus clause and its fossilised form: la ṣa – v-ṛṣ 'to spray'. The derivative v-ṛ́ṣ-an and its immediate meaning 'bull' may serve as clue for the meaning of this clause. What does a bull do? It impregnates the herd.

If ṣa (embryo) is the object, la may be the verb. Because the order is reversed, it is in the passive voice. Perhaps la ṣa means: the eggs are hatched. It might be a taboo for the cattle-breeding centre where animals were brought together for mating.

37

The Village-well

One of the words for 'water' in the RV is udán, later also extended as uda-ká, said to be derived from ud (u-na-t-ti u-n-d-anti) 'to water, wet'. The same root is there in sam-ud-ra 'sea'. The word uda- occurs in certain compounds (lavaṇoda, uda-bindu, etc.). Perhaps there was also the noun *úd 'water', later extended as út-sa 'well', -sa being rather a word from san 'to get' than a suffix, the word originally meaning 'procuring water'.

In the Indus inscriptions there is a text va ṭha . Phonetically it may have been reduced to úd, just as we have vanád 'fire' from va ṇa ṭha, nod (analysed in the pada-text as na + ud), of uncertain meaning, from ṇa va ṭha. The text va (water) ṭha (circle) is a clause: there is water in the circle. Later, it was a phrase: the water in the circle, referring to the village-well of circular shape, where the water was stored for the domestic use. It should have been in the centre of the village. We have such wells even now in the remote villages.

Even now the village-wells are circular in shape and are deep upto the level of the water under the earth. Perhaps the well was popularly known as 'the water in the circle'. The storing of water for other purposes, e.g. irrigation, etc. would have been in the form of reservoirs of various shapes and sizes, but the village-wells were always circular and smaller in size, because they were man-made.

Even now the waters are carried to distant places in the countryside through ḍhos from the natural reservoirs and through another instrument called ḍhekul from the wells.

The Indus texts gradually reveal to us that it was just the beginning of a human civilisation in the Indus valley.

38

The Agriculture Started

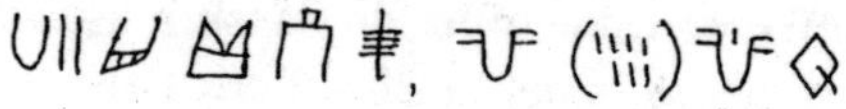

This two-line text is hardly comprehensible at the first sight. But let us try to read it to comprehend its purport.

The first line is familiar through its ṣu and ṣa at the end of the first and second clause respectively. They are supposed to be two bisyllabic clauses connected with 'if'. The first sign, a c-syllable, can be read cā, if the first clause reflects in the colloquial cās (a piece of cultivable land). In Santhali, cās means 'cultivation' and cāsā means 'cultivator'. The second clause of the first line reflects in rustic word ḍhos (a siphoning instrument in the countryside used nowadays). Then the first line may be read thus: cā ṣu ḍho ṣa, meaning: if the cultivable land becomes dry, the (stored) water should be siphoned in.

The reading of the second line is very uncertain, specially on the first and third signs, and the meaning is then naturally more uncertain. Though every sign has some provisional phonetic value in our mind on account of a long association with the Indus script, the first sign reading e/o and the third sign reading tha is still very uncertain. The meaning of the first clause is then more uncertain. Let us leave it for the time being.

The last three signs read: ha ra ga. The last syllable ga is an injunctive affix, and the preceding ra is then naturally a verb. But if the first two syllables ha ra reflect in hala (a ploughing instrument in the countryside), ha-ra is a bisyllabic verb, meaning 'to plough'. Perhaps the last clause says: plough the land.

Now the first clause of the second line seems to give some sense. Perhaps e is the pronoun 'this' bu = rain, and tha = uncertain. That is to say, the clause means: the rain is uncertain.

Because the Indus people had to depend on monsoon for their agricultural activities, they had to issue some instructions from time to time to the peasants: As soon as the cultivable land becomes dry, the stored water should be siphoned in. The rain is uncertain. Before the land becomes dry, it should be furrowed.

The verb śuṣ (to dry up) seems to have developed from some *cuṣ with the affricate value of /c/. In Sanskrit itself, there is a verb cūṣ (to suck up), which is not much different also semantically. At the isolating stage of Indus, cu ṣa should have been some clause.

39

Lavatory System

A text 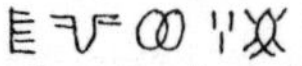 ha ga cha ṣa gha seems to have two clauses: ha-ga, cha ṣa-gha. Though ha has not been assigned the meaning 'faeces' in the traditional lexicons of the monosyllabic words*, we infer from the modern rustic dialects that ha-ga means: do defecate! The syllable cha of the next clause stands for 'disgust, distaste' (colloquially, there is chi), redolent of some lavatory system in that society proceeding towards urbanization. The clause perhaps says: the smell is indeed there. People were advised to use it.

Perhaps it was a sign-board on the gate of some lavatory system. Mike Edwards, reporting on the excavations at Harappa in Pakistan under Richard Meadow and Mark Kennoyer, believes that there were toilets with brick supports for seats. Effluent sluiced to a brick-lined sewer or to a buried urn. (National Geographic, Vol. 197, No. 6, June 2000, p. 126). Meadow believed that the Indus people were quite advanced in their toilet arrangements.

The verb hag- (pronounced exactly like the Eng. hug) is used in the rustic dialects throughout India in the sense of 'defecation', though in the polite language various terms have been coined to avoid disgust.

---

* Some meanings of ha are obscure; e.g. nakulīśa.

40

Storing Waters

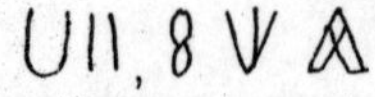

ī va ta, ra-ga

This text was partly examined earlier (1997: From Indus to Sanskrit, Pt. III, p. 96). The phonetic identification of the first three signs was then as provisional as it is even now. The first sign is the long ī on the basis of the simple form ∧ standing for i, even diacritically in  ri. The second sign is va on account of V being used diacritically for u in  yu. And the identification of the third sign as ta is purely a guesswork on the basis of the whole group ī va ta appearing to reflect in an obscure and controversial Vedic vocable īvat.

The exact meaning of īvat perhaps may reveal the meaning of the Indus clause ī va ta. On the other hand, this clause itself may shed some light on the possibly more exact meaning of īvat in the following RVedic passages:

īvate brahmaṇe	4, 4, 6
īvato' gneḥ	4, 15, 5
īvato dyūn	4, 43, 3
īvat … namas	5, 49, 5
īvate janāya	6, 73, 2
īvato me	7, 23, 1
īvat pūrtam	8, 46, 21

Because īvat is an adjective of bráhman (prayer), agni (fire) div (day), namas (greeting), jana (people), me (of me), and pūrtam (present), it may be having the meanings pleasant, bright, agreeable, loving, or the like. The three syllables of the clause may have combined to bring out such meanings in course of a long history.

Perhaps Sāyaṇa had rightly perceived ī as a pronominal base, ī = it, which is also acceptable to Geldner. It is only on the next syllable that they differ, they go apart, each in the wrong direction. The next syllable -vat is the reduced form of -vata, = va ta of the Indus text, on account of the accent on the first syllable.

The syllable va means 'water', and ta has 'womb' as one of the meanings. The clause ī va ta then seems to mean: it stores waters, or, the waters are stored in it, perhaps referring to some big reservoir of the waters. That is why, the following clause, ra (love) – ga, advises: care for its safety! The reservoir of the waters was a boon for the people. It helped agriculture and supported the life of the citizens.

After a considerable interval, during which the clause ī va ta had contracted as īvat and the meaning had turned into unpredictable directions, the 'prayer' became agreeable, the fire 'comfortable', the day 'bright', the greeting 'polite', people 'worthy of beneficial deeds', 'I' loving, and the present 'pleasant'.

The editors of the pada-text did not analyse īvat, but the compilers of the monosyllabic words saw Lakṣmī (wealth, beauty), Kāma (love) in ī, because they could have understood īvat as 'beneficial, beautiful'.

Mike Edwards (National Geographic, June 2000, p. 129) had observed numerous reservoirs scattered about Dholavira and the archaeologist RS Bisht had opined that 'the people were thinking not to let a single drop of water escape'.

41

The Reservoir of Water

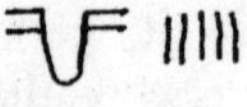

ca ṣa

This little text reflects in Sanskrit caṣaka 'cup', which is just an extension of the original caṣa-. The latest meaning 'cup' seems to refer to some 'reservoir of waters'. That is to say, at some earlier stage of the language, this caṣa was a phrase, meaning 'containing waters'. Naturally, at the isolating stage of the language, it was a clause: (it) contains water, both ca (water) and ṣa (to hold, contain) having new connotations in our glossary.

Another text 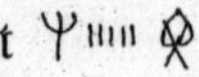 ṇa ca ṇa has perhaps the same meaning 'water' for ca. The syllable ṇa, being the basis of the Vedic verb an 'to breathe', perhaps means 'a living being' in the first case and has some appropriate verbal idea in the second. The meaning of the text may be this: for the living beings (plants and animals) the water is life. We may suppose that /c/ is an affricate and, with the preceding ṇa, it has turned up naś (to perish) in Sanskrit. Naturally, without the water the life perishes. That is to say, the Vedic verb naś has evolved from ṇa ca (one is alive through the water). This is the linguistic embryology.

The colloquial vāṭī and kaṭorī 'cup' (water-container) of the kitchen of the countryside preserves the sense of water in va and ka, the following sounds ṭ and r having some appropriate sense.

The text  va ci, if read correctly, may be interpreted with the appropriate meaning of v and c. On the basis of the affricate value of /c/, we may suppose that vas (to dwell) has evolved from va (dwelling) ci (water), which may be supposed to mean: the water should be stored. In the village dialects, cavacā is a 'little pool of waters'.

Two more texts are well readable, but the interpretation may be only speculative.

1360 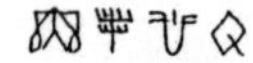 cā ṣu la ṭha

4536  h̲a da cā ṣa

The second clause of the first text has finally evolved as ṛtá (the regular order of the universe) with its diverse later meanings. The first clause reflects in the colloquial cās 'cultivable land'. But the two clauses coming together do not give any suitable meaning. A different text cā ṣu ḍho ṣa means: if the land is dry, siphon waters (into it). Perhaps, as elsewhere, la ṭha has the usual meaning: the time turns round. The whole text perhaps says: if the land has become dry, the time turns round (wait for the arrival of the rains).

The second text reflects in sad (to languish) and cās. Perhaps h̲a (sky) da (heat) says: the sky is hot; the land is drying up. It may refer to drought.

From these statements we learn that the Indus communities were coming to farming and agriculture. This was the early stage of the Indus culture.

The Indus clauses in isolation have turned up as reduced vocables with distantly related meanings in the language of the RV. But there is no instance of the whole text being reduced to vocables with related meanings. A characteristic feature of the texts of the Indus inscriptions is that it is always a clause, even if there is only one sign. Our Sanskrit grammarians had some idea of this prehistoric language, because they have defined a clause as 'having a verb' (eka-tiṅ vākyam).

42

The Perennial Waters from the Mountain

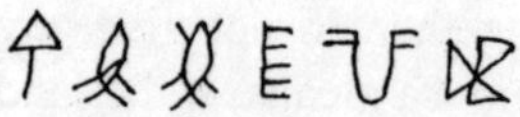

yo ṣa-gha, ha ma ṣa

The reading of the text is not doubtless, the first sign from the right itself being doubtful. The sign  also, on which the sound-value of  has been based, is not free from doubt.

The text seems to have two clauses, the first terminating at the future affix -gha: yo ṣa-gha. If yo has the usually assumed meaning 'happiness', the clause says: there will be happiness. Though there is no clear indication, the following clause may be syntactically related with it through some conjunction.

The clause yo ṣa (-gha) has fossilised as yós (comfort), often used with śám (wellbeing): śáṃ yóḥ, śáṃ ca yóś ca. The next clause ha ma ṣa may be supposed to have fossilised phonetically as haṃsá (goose, swan), which has also a number of meanings recorded in the traditional Sanskrit lexicons. Those unattested meanings of the lexicons cannot be ignored, because they are also based on some lost tradition. There are many factors for the imposition of a meaning on a word. The radical meaning is often retained.

One of the lexical meaning of haṃsá is 'mountain'. Because the first monosyllabic word of a clause retains its meaning when the clause is reduced to a lexeme, the meaning 'mountan' may be attached to ha itself. Thus ha ma ṣa seems to say: from the mountain (ha) the waters (ma) come (ṣa). Then this clause is not much different from another clause ṣa ra ṣa (from the nipple = mountain flows and stops at the sea), which has fossilised as sáras (pond, lake), being responsible for the name Saras-vat-ī (abounding in ponds) of the same river. It is due to the identity of the referend of the two clauses that the river Saraswatī, on the banks of which the Vedic culture began to flourish, later deified as the goddess of learning, is made to ride on the water-bird swan referred to by the fossilised haṃsá from the clause ha ma ṣa. In the RV, haṃsá is the vehicle of the Aśvins, later of Brahmā also, and it shows that there was a big gap of time between the Indus and the Vedic cultures. But haṃsa meaning 'horse', 'draught ox' and also 'buffalo' is just a transfer of meaning from 'swan' as vehicle.

Then the whole text yo ṣa-gha, ha ma ṣa may be said to say like this: there will be happiness (among the people), because the waters come from the mountain. That is to say, it was not the rain-water, which is temporary and uncertain, but it is the perennial waters from the mountain.

We may go a step further and presume that this statement was issued on the occasion of some canal being dug out from the main river. Because the swan and other aquatic birds had come to inhabit those peaceful waters of the canal, the fossilised form haṃsa began to refer to them.

If what we have said above is correct, the first sign of the text really reads yo. That is to say, the reading of the text is correct.

43

The Soma-juice

h̲aō ma ṣu dhe ṣa ra ci bu

This text was taken up earlier in 1997 (From Indus to Sanskrit, Pt. III, p. 103). But it had not been read correctly. However, syntactically, the text was somewhat understood. The verb ṣa bent towards ṣu in the first clause shows the syntactic relation with the following clause. Further, the verb ra put before the qualified object indicates a passive construction. The syllabic group ci bu intentionally put in two lines may be the object with specific qualification.

Perḥaps the graphic form of the text has been now understood correctly. A symbolic translation of the text may be the following.

There is ma in h̲aō; it is dhe. ra (verb) ci (adj.) bu (object).

The syllabic group h̲aō ma later contracted as sóma (Av. haoma) 'the soma plant'. The next clause dhe ṣa was fossilised as dhiṣ (intellect) in the RV, used only in instrumental: dhiṣā (mindfully, zealously). The last three syllables have never come together.

A workable translation of the text may be the following:

There is water (ma) in the plant (h̲aō); it is intoxicating (dhe). The shining (ci) juice (bu) is strained (ra).

The plant was the same as was later called h̲aōma > Vedic Soma Av. haoma. The juice pressed out of this plant has been described as intoxicating. This soma juice was mixed with milk on account of which it became white. When the soma plants were crushed by stone, the juice was mixed with water and milk and strained through cloth. These are the few ideas which have been expressed in this little text.

This Indus text is the first reference for the intoxicating Soma drink of the Vedic cult. It may be supposed that the Indus people came to know about the soma plants as soon as they turned to farming and other hard works. This continued with them till it became a part of the rituals of the soma sacrifice of the Vedic culture.

As we go on reading the texts, we find everything here in its primitive form which is elaborated later. Sometimes the ideas remained the same, but they were expressed differently later. Thus ẖa (horse) was extended as ẖa-ś-va > aśva, also replaced by ghoṭa, ambā (mother) was replaced by mātar, and so on.

If madhu (honey) is to be associated with the Soma juice, it may be supposed to have travelled to Central Asia and Europe, because Gk. has methu, Anglo-Saxon medu, Eng. mead.

44

To Look Inward and to See with Eyes

2369 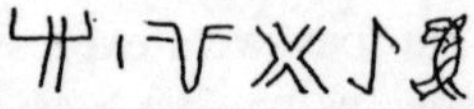

śa ma yo ṣa pa śa

The two-third of the present text, that is, śa ma yo ṣa, has already been examined elsewhere. Though the following pa śa of the present text could have been taken up immediately thereafter, there was no clue to break the code. This pa śa also forms a part of some other texts, often in varying graphic forms, that is  and . But these are not to be considered here.

This clause seems to reflect in a controversial form paḍ-bhis (RV 4, 2, 12), analysed in the pada-text as pad-bhis and accepted by Sāyaṇa and Geldner, but conceived by Roth as from some prehistoric paś meaning 'eye'. On its face-value, paś may be the phonetically fossilised form of the Indus clause pa śa, which may be interpreted only through the former.

Though Geldner follows Sāyaṇa regarding the meaning of paś, he differs from him in putting dṛśyām paḍbhis parallel to adbhutān evais, whereas Sāyaṇa puts them in one line, paḍbhis qualified by evais.

If the RVedic form paḍbhis is genuine, the emendation of the pada-text is unjustified and both Sāyaṇa and Geldner are wrong. Then Roth's view about the base paś- and its meaning 'eye' is to be critically examined.

The clause pa śa of the isolating stage could have come together and paśa would have been a bisyllabic verb at the agglutinative stage. Here an s-was prefixed to it with some supposed distinction in the original meaning, which is retained even at the inflexional stage in the past participle s-paṣ-ṭá, probably meaning 'seen physically with the eyes'.

In the present system of the Vedic conjugation, the prefixed s-was dropped (paś-ya-ti, etc.), and even elsewhere it is never to be seen, but Roth's paś is exactly this spaś with slight modification in the meaning. Perhaps the inflexional spaś = to see physically, and the agglutinative paśa = to see inward. Thus paś (noun) = inward looking, inner vision, insight. Let us interpret the RV 4, 2, 12 cd with this meaning of paś:

Therefore, o Agni, the noble one, you see the visible and the invisible ones with quick (eva) insight (paś).

That is to say, because paś means 'insight', pa śa may be supposed to mean: see inside (through the mind's eye), see the invisible, what the Vedic singer says.

Perhaps the fossilised paś was on the death-bed already in the oldest language of the RV. Therefore, the later singers did not conceive anything other than pad (foot) even in the older forms. Consequently, even in paḍ-gṛbhi (RV 10, 49, 5) and paḍ-bīśa (1, 162, 4) only pad- is conceived to be hidden.

In respect of the language from Vedic to Sanskrit, Böhtlingk and Roth say: ... "From there the thread of ideas runs which can be grasped exactly when its beginning is determined. Or, where in the later language the basic meaning of a word deviates, is evidently broken asunder in disconnected pieces, like an used up or effaced coin, that can be seen in the treasure of the Veda.

Many roots, which disappear later, rich word-families which have been left over with poor descendants, are lively here in blooming state". (Vorwort: Sanskrit - Wörterbuch).

The same remark may be carried back to the Indus language from where Sanskrit had started its journey.

45

The Generation of Light

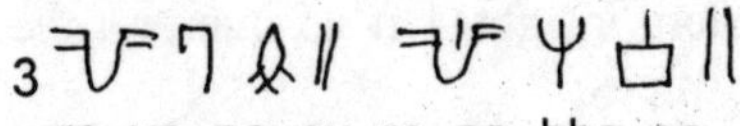

ra va ṇa ṣu ra na bha ṣa

There is no doubt about the reading of the text, but the interpretation is highly uncertain. It was examined, sometimes partly sometimes fully, on pages 106, 122, 130 in the third part, From Indus to Sanskrit (1997). But the interpretation was not satisfactory.

The structure of the text is remarkably usual: ṣu at the end of the first clause and ṣa at the end of the second. This at least suggests the relationship of the two clauses through some conjunction: ra va ṇa ṣu – ra na bha ṣa.

The glossary of the monosyllabic words states the following meanings of each of them:

ra	=	fire
va	=	water
ṇa	=	breath (= steam)
ṣa	=	embryo (to generate)
na	=	gem
bha	=	light

The syllable ra occurs in the two clauses, supposedly having the same or two fairly identical meanings. A symbolic interpretation may be this: ra and va generate ṇa, (and) ra and na generate bha.

If ra in both the clauses is in the oblique case, va ṇa ṣu and na bha ṣa may be subject + object + verb : through the fire the water generates steam (and) through the heat the gem generates light. The conjunction connecting the two clauses may be 'as' or 'so': as through the fire the water generates steam, (so) through the heat the gem generates light.

In this connection, it is relevant to quote a scientific truth from the Children's Encyclopaedia by Arthur Mee, p. 4099:

> "When cold, it (= the carbon) gives out no light and does not reflect much; but heat it up and it first grows red, and then as it grows hotter, it can be made to give out a white light, as in electric arc-lamp."

In our glossary, na stands for 'gem', but in the modern terminology it could be carbon too, because both are after all matters.

46

There is Life After Death

ma ṇu ṣa

There is some aoubt on the reading of the text on the second syllable. But, most probably, it has been correctly read ṇu, because only on the basis of this reading we may be able to reach a fossilised Vedic vacable manus 'a human being', also extended to mánuṣ-a and manuṣ-yá.

Previously, in a longer text bū jña ṣu ma ṇu ṣa the same ma ṇu ṣa was interpreted thus: death is certain, because the subordinate clause preceding it appeared to say: if the sewer water (bū) is contaminated (jña). (The RV in the Indus inscriptions, 2003, p. 128-29). In modern Persian bū has, therefore, acquired the meaning 'smell' from the 'contaminated water'.

In the same clause appearing independently, the meaning may slightly change, ma (end) ṇu (life) ṣa (embryo) appearing to say: the end makes a (new) beginning. That is to say, after a man dies, he is born again.

As a matter of fact, this meaning may be carried to the longer text also: as the sewer water is contaminated, the end makes a new beginning. Here it seems to be a taboo for the possible death due to the contaminated water. The idea of death has been expressed in a suggestive way: the contaminated water may cause the beginning of an end. They had realised that the death is a sad event; therefore, it should not be uttered abruptly.

We see that though the language is still at the isolating stage, their thoughts are wiser. They had realised the highest truth that there is life after death. On the Vedic pattern, we derive manus 'a man' from man 'to think', but really a man is one who is destined to die as soon as he is born. The Indus inscriptions are making us wiser even linguistically.

47

The Vedic Carṣaṇí

The meaning of carṣaṇí is controversial on account of its doubtful etymology. As an adjective, it is said to mean 'active, agile, swift'. As a feminine noun in pl., it is said to mean 'men, people'. Monier-Williams sees the root kṛṣ 'to cultivate' in it and he thinks that originally it means 'cultivator', who is 'active or agile' with its adjectival meaning, and is 'opposed to nomads' with its nominal meaning 'men, people'. Roth sees the root car 'to go' in it, while the traditional commentators connect it with cakṣ 'to see'. Its compound with -dhṛ́ti and -sáh also does not throw any light on the original meaning.

Its initial element carṣ- may be theoretically conceived as the reduced form of cánas (pleasure, delight, satisfaction, with dhā meaning 'to delight in, enjoy') on the analogy of vánas > varṣ, tánas > tarṣ, and many others. Theoretically, this cánas may be expanded to the size of the Indus clause ca na ṣa. Fortunately, there is also ca ṇa ṣa in the Indus inscriptions. The clause ca ṇa ṣa 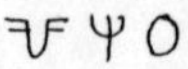 is imaginable through ca ṇa ṣu va ṇa ṣa 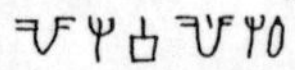 and ca na ṣa 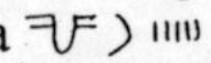 is attested through rau ṇa ca na ṣa 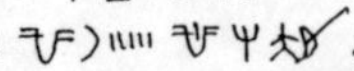.

Both ca ṇa ṣa and ca na ṣa have converged as cánas in the Vedic language. Two meanings in cánas are not discernible in the Vedic occurrences, but its further reduction to carṣ- in carṣ-aṇ-í has certainly two meanings, as indicated above. The adjectival meaning should reflect in one clause and the nominal meaning in another. That is to say, one clause was fossilised as adjective and the other as noun in cánas in the later phase of the language. It is true that only the central syllables ṇa and na make the difference. Though the difference is obscure at the cánas stage, it should have been clearly evident at *carṣ- stage.

If ca = moon, then ṇa = knowledge, intelligence, appears to be cogent, taking into account the relation of 'moon' and 'mind'. Then ca ṇa ṣa = the moon gives knowledge or the moon is intelligence, may be the possible meaning. If ca = thief, then na = gem, appears to be reasonable, because ca na ṣa = the thief takes away the gem, is a possible meaning.

The clause ca ṇa ṣa would have become cánas meaning 'knowledge, intelligence' and would have required its extension through the suffix -aṇ-i to make it mean 'intelligent'. This meaning has been suggested by Burnouf. It has no connection with car (Roth), cakṣ (Yāska) or kṛṣ (MW).

The clause ca na ṣa too would have become cánas meaning 'theft, robbery'. It reduced form carṣ- meaning * 'wealth' (which could be stolen or robbed) would have required its extension through -aṇ-i meaning 'wealthy people', which might be applicable to 'people' in general.

This carṣ-aṇ-i has logically two different meanings, adj. 'intelligent' and noun 'people', because it has come from two different sources in the ur-Sprache.

48

An Engineer : nisará

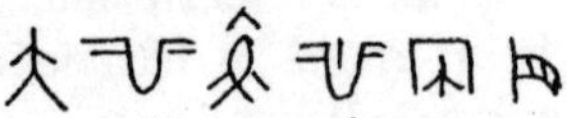

ra ghī ṣu ni ṣa ra

The second sign of this text had been read jī earlier to identify a Vedic word ṛjīṣa (of controversial meaning) in the Indus inscriptions. Then  has to be read ja, which has been read gha elsewhere. Because gha also is not attested through some Vedic word,  has been taken to be a sign for ja. An earlier from of this sign in the list of variants is , which prompts us to see gha in it through the rustic words ghẽṭ (neck), ghegh (thyroid gland), ghogh (throat) representing this sign. If this sign is gh after all,  may be read ghī, but it may be supposed to have become jī through palatalisation and deaspiration in Vedic.

The syllable gha means 'heat'. Thus the first clause ra ghī ṣu seems to mean: when the fire causes heat ..., and ni ṣa ra, a passive construction (the object before the verb) means: in the interior the speed is caused. Perhaps ra has two symbols only to distinguish two meanings (fire: speed). It relates to some fire engine, the machine caused to move through heat. The second clause ni ṣa ra appears to have fossilised without any phonetic decay as nisará with a very obscure meaning in VS 3, 14:

manyave ayas-tāpám	(for manyu an iron-smith)
krodhāya nisarám	(for krodha ? nisara).

In a straightforward way, the whole text seems to say: as the fire causes heat, there is motion inside. The 'motion inside caused by the heat' should reflect in some 'professional' later, similar to iron-smith, e.g. an engineer. Then, in the Vedic context, nisará = a controller, pacifier, solicitor.

It appears that all the clauses of the Indus inscriptions have been preserved in the Vedic language in form of the fossilised words with their obscure meanings. When the culture of a society changes, its language also changes with high and long jumps in unpredictable direction.

49

The Transition of Thoughts

Now three texts are taken up to show how the thoughts of the agrarian Indus people were changing their levels. Not long ago, they had started farming through the facilities provided by nature. Because they were intelligent people, they also began to distinguish the different objects of nature through their action. Though they had a limited amount of vocabulary at their disposal, the same word could be used for different objects according to situation. The different subjects could change the meaning of the same word for object. The three texts are the following:

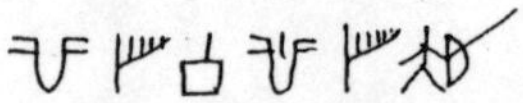

rau dha ṣu va dha ṣa

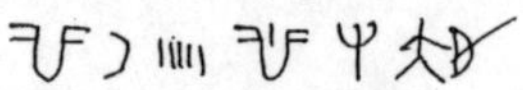

rau ṇa ṣu ca na ṣa

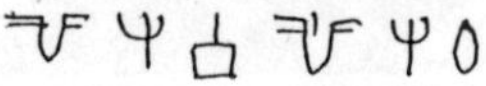

ca ṇa ṣu va ṇa ṣa

The first text has been discussed in a previous book "The RV in the Indus inscriptions" (2003), p. 125. The meaning "if the sun is hot, the rain is in plenty" betrays the actual experience of the Indus farmers, who were engaged in agriculture a short while ago.

The fossilised form of the first clause reflects in the modern colloquial raüdā 'the heat of the sun'. The same of the second clause reflects in the verb vadh 'to kill', because sometimes the plenty of rain was not less than a 'killer'.

The second text appears to distinguish the action of the sun (rau) and the moon (ca). The object of the action of the sun is perhaps the animal life (ṇa) and the same of the moon is the plant life (na). The text appears to mean: just as the sun gives energy to animals, the moon gives energy to plants. It is based on the keen observation of nature on a higher level. From seeing they had proceeded towards imagination.

In the third text, the action of the 'fire' and 'water' are distinguished. Both ca ṇa ṣa and va ṇa ṣa of the text have respectively fossilised as cánas and vánas and, further, as carṣ in carṣ-aṇ-í (1. a wiseman, cultivator 2. wise, intelligent) and varṣ/vṛṣ (to rain). The word cánas generally precedes the verb dhā, canodadhāti meaning 'likes, accepts, finds pleasure in'. Thus cánas is something like 'agreeableness, pleasure'. The word vánas is just the first idea (water-cultured) in vánas-páti (plant), but elsewhere it is also said to mean 'loveliness', which is just a transfer of meaning, because plants are of course lovely. There is rain-fall because of plants on the earth, and vṛṣ has naturally resulted from vánas.

The derivative carṣ-aṇ-í is a noun in some case and an adjective in some other, because carṣ from cánas itself has come from two clauses, ca ṇa ṣa and ca na ṣa, in Indus. The clause ca ṇa ṣa means: the fire gives comfort to human beings. And ca na ṣa means: the oyster produces pearls. In this case, we have the Indus clause ca ṇa ṣa. The second word ṇa in the two clauses may differ in meaning only on account of the different subjects, ca (fire) and va (water), at the beginning. Perhaps the text means: as the fire (ca) gives comfort (ṇa) to human beings, the water (va) gives life (ṇa) to plants.

Because the exact meanings of the monosyllabic words are not known, we are just beating around the bush. An exact and definite meaning is never in sight, except in a few rare cases.

50

At the Beginning of the Creation

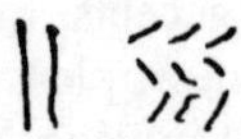

The text doubtlessly reads: sa ra. It is either a clause of the type subject + verb or a verb in the pluperfect form.

In the first case, sa + ra does not make any sensible clause with the quotable meanings of sa and ra in the traditional lexicons of the monosyllabic words. If sa- is a verb with the pluperfect affix -ra, a passage of the RV (10, 129, 3 b) seems to suggest what it may mean: a-praketaṃ salilaṃ sarvam ā idam (Indistinguishable it was water all over). That is to say, (a-praketaṃ) salilaṃ (sarvam) āḥ seems to be equal to sa-ra, where sa = (a-praketaṃ) salilam (water) and -ra = āḥ, that is, āsīt (had been). The paraphrasing is almost verbatim, the base and suffix distinctly explained. The Vedic salilá also means 'sea'. Manusmṛti says: apa eva sasarjādau (He created waters first of all).

While etymologizing sarit 'stream, river', Prof. Thieme had rejected its connection with sṛ (to move). He had analysed it as sar + i-t (from i 'to go'). The first element sar- is the same as sal- in saline from the Latin sal (salt). That is to say, sar-it means: going to the saline waters, i.e. sea.

Thus the Indus text seems to say: it had been (saline) waters (everywhere), and it has been faithfully paraphrased by the singers of the RV. We may suppose that sa = (saline) water, sea at the isolating stage of Indus. As a matter of fact, even salilá is just an extension of sal- from the pluperfect form sa-ra (it had been saline water). We see how a word of the Indus origin is readily connected with a Vedic verb.

We also see that this text is exclusively in the numeral script, which is the latest phase in the development of the Indus script. The cosmogonic ideas are not the product of only the latest phase of the RV. They are present in their primitive form even at the border of the isolating and agglutinative Indus. The ideas were floating under currently from the beginning of the Indus culture. The Vedic singers describe the creation as if they had seen it with their own eyes.

The Vedic singers are said to be mantra-draṣṭāraḥ. They had seen the algebrical statements of the early stages of Indus. When they had become too incomprehensible, they expanded the old sayings in the inflexional stage of the language of the same stream. We call it the Vedic language. For them, it was the grand-child of the old grand-mother.

51

Reason Followed Instinct

1092 rau ṇa ṣu ca na ṣa 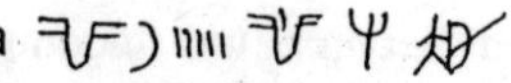

2263 ca ṇa ṣu va ṇa ṣa 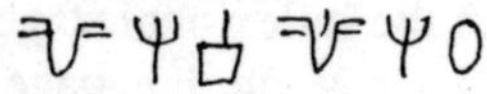

These two texts were examined, one after another, in 1997 (From Indus to Sanskrit, Pt. III, 52-3). Though the reading was doubtlessly correct, in interpretation it was a total failure, in spite of the fact that the fossils of these Indus clauses, namely: *róṇas cánas vánas, were traced in the Vedic language.

They were taken up in the same sequence in 2000 (The evolution of the Indus language and its transition into Sanskrit, pp. 58-9). The fossilised forms of the four clauses of the two texts were traced deeper to carṣ- in carṣ-aṇ-í and varṣ (= vṛṣ 'to rain). Though the successive phonetic decay of the Indus clauses was transparently clear, in meanings there was a frog's jump in unpredicted directions. As a matter of fact, the meanings were totally mutilated, carried to unimaginable destinations. Though ca ṇa ṣu and ca na ṣa have converged as cánas in Vedic, its further decayed form carṣ- in carṣ-aṇ-í has been distinguished semantically, the latter being a noun in one case and an adjective in another. But there was no further breakthrough in meaning.

The same two texts were examined once more in 2003 (The RV in Indus inscriptions, p. 127), but any breakthrough in meaning was not achieved. However, carṣ-aṇ-í was semantically specified as 1. (the wealthy) people (noun) and 2. wise, intelligent (adjective). It was also made clear that all the Vedic words cannot be derived from the Vedic roots; they have their roots even at a deeper level.

The central syllable ṇa in three clauses and na in the fourth have been the source of trouble. It is supposed that ṇa differs in meaning according as it is preceded by rau, ca and va.

Because rau is 'sun' and ca is 'moon', ṇa in rau ṇa ṣu means 'breath' or 'life' and na in ca na ṣa means 'mind'. In this connection, Sir Arthur Mee's Children's encyclopaedia offers a remarkable clue to the possible meaning: ... "many thousands of years after life in myriad form had appeared ..., there came into existence a creature different from any other creature under the shining sun ... . This creature had a mind." Based on this, the clauses may be said to mean: the sun created life (long ago); the moon created mind (later).

In ca ṇa ṣu va ṇa ṣa, the same ṇa is preceded by ca and va. It is reasonable to suppose that ṇa has two meanings in the two clauses. In this connection, the RV 10, 90, 13 candramā manaso jātaḥ (the moon was born from the mind) and vāyuḥ prāṇād ajāyata (the air was born from the breath) as well as TS 5, 1, 5, 1 prāṇo vai vāyuḥ (the air is the breath) are comparable. Perhaps the Indus clauses say: the moon is intelligence; the air is breath. In another context, va ṇa ṣa means: from the water the life comes.

The bending of the verb in the first clause towards u is just a trick to connect two clauses. It is said that the primitive communities changed their vocabulary from generation to generation.

The translation of the two texts may be thus finally redrafted (Long ago) the sun created life; (then) the moon added mind (to it). The moon is intelligence; the air is life.

52

The Ṛbhus of the RV

4121 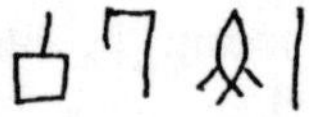

la na bha-va

The reading of the text appears to be doubtless. It is only the meaning which makes us falter at every syllable and on the whole text.

The syllable la is intimately related with 'time' in meaning, because it is authenticated by Pāṇini. Though ka itself means time, la was added to its strengthened form kā (in kāla) to suggest its eternity. The compound dik-kāla stands for the 'infinite time and space', and this concept was very familiar to the Indus Aryans.

The meaning 'unbroken' for na in the lexicons is just symbolic. It suggests the infinity and continuity of the time-concept.

The last two syllables bha va are the original elements of what later developed as the root bhu (i.e. bhū) 'to be'. The extension of bha by ra ultimately resulted in bhṛ 'to bear', by ya in bhi (i.e. bhī) 'to fear', by ja in bhaj 'to cook' (cf. its voiceless version pac), by ṇa in bhaṇ 'to say', by da in bhad cf. bhad-ra 'good'), by ṣa in bhaṣ 'to bark', in bhāṣ 'to speak', by sa in bhas 'to burn' in bhas-man 'ashes', bhas-trā 'a bellows'. These extended forms reveal the original sense in bha on the one hand and in ya, ra, ja, ṇa, da, sa and sa on the other, although the transfer of meaning has taken place in unpredictable way and any guess is hazardous.

The text la na bha va seems to say: the time is continuous, eternal or infinite. The clause later seems to have contracted as lamb 'to hang down' with various associated meanings. We may not also doubt its being at the root of ṛbhú. The bisyllabic group la na has contracted as ra and bha-va as bhu which, bearing accent, reduced ra to ṛ. Briefly, ṛbhú is the 'time' personified, the Vedic version of the classical Kāla-puruṣa.

53

The Vedic rātá- and rātí

The word rātá appears as the first member of the compounds rātá-manas 'having a willing mind', rātá-havis and -havya 'willingly offering presents'. There is also rātí adj. 'willing to offer' and noun fem. 'a will to offer'. Following the Vedic etymological pattern, it is derived from rā 'to give'. The meaning hardly seems to be questionable. Even arāti (a non-giver) 'enemy' seems to justify the proposed meaning.

In the corpus of the Indus texts, there is 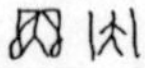, read rā ṭha, once preceded by la , once by la na 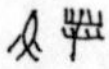, and once by 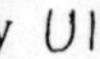 ya ga. Besides, there is also a text 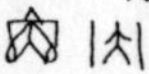 rā ṭhi. We have noticed elsewhere in the Indus texts that ṭha is represented by ta in Vedic: ṣa ṭha > sát, va ṇa ṭha > vart, etc. Therefore, we may suppose the Indus rā ṭha and rā ṭhi to have emerged as rātá and rātí in Vedic. Because the accent has rested on the final syllable and the first syllable bears the long vowel ā, the word has remained intact in passing from Indus to Vedic in this case.

This correspondence of the vedic rātá rātí and the Indus rā ṭha rā ṭhi makes us suspect the accepted meanings of the Vedic words. Let us, first of all, attempt the interpretation of the Indus texts.

If rā ṭha and rā ṭhi are clauses of the type s + v, it may mean: fire (ra) disc (ṭha), that is, some shining object turns round. It may refer to the 'revolution of the moon around the earth'. It is not strange that rātá is the adjective of manas (mind) intimately connected with the moon, as well as of havis and havya which shines due to the clarified butter. Thus rātá may really mean 'pure' or 'clear'. That is to say, rātá-manas = having a pure mind, rātá-havis/havya = having lustrous oblation.

Even rātí may similarly mean lustrous (adj.) and lustre (noun). That is to say, the verb rā 'to give' should not be brought in this context. These words were already there before the verb rā could evolve in the Vedic language.

Thus rātá and rātí as adjective mean 'pure, clear, lustrous'. As a noun rātí should mean 'purity, lustre'. Because we try to derive every Vedic word from the Vedic material, we are led astray, even though the meaning appears justified in the new generation of the language.

54

The Big Gap between the Indus and Vedic Cultures

2687 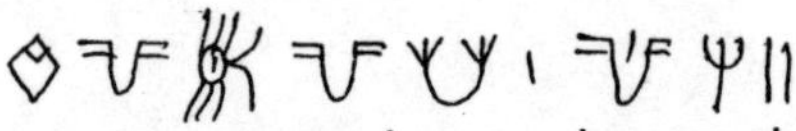

ra ṇa ṣu pa ka ṣa bu ṣa ci

This text was taken up earlier in 2000 for examination (The Indus language, p. 60). A workable but unsatisfactory interpretation was put forward. Though the reading of the text is the same, doubtlessly correct, the meaning may be revised here, and also again in future.

The fossilised Vedic form of the first clause may be *ráṇas, but that is unattested. A shorter form ráṇa is there, to be discussed later below. In its crude form, the clause ra ṇa ṣa (fire knowledge embryo) seems to say: from the fire there is knowledge. A Rvedic verse of identical intention says: agninā rayim aśnavat (Through Agni one may get wealth). To make the Indus clause and the Vedic verse agree, ṇa in the traditional lexicons is 'gift'. Then, ra ṇa ṣa = From the fire there is wealth. Though it may be satisfactory with respect to the singers of the RV, it is still unsatisfactory with reference to the Indus culture.

The earliest meaning of the shorter form ráṇa, that is, 'joy, comfort, desire' and its radical element ran 'to feel well, be comfortable, rejoice at' may help to arrive at a more exact meaning, i.e.: the fire brings forth comfort (through its warmth). It is possibly the most cogent meaning of the first clause in respect of a primitive community. In the present text, this clause is syntactically connected with the following two clauses, as shown by the verb bent towards u.

The second clause pa ka ṣa (air joy embryo) seems to have fossilised as pakṣá 'wing, side' in Vedic, and its vulgar form is paṃkhā (fan) in Hindi. This clause seems to say: in the air there is coolness.

The last clause bu ṣa ci (rain embryo light), the verb put before the object, perhaps means: the rain is accompanied by the lightning.

The whole text now seems to say: As the fire gives warmth, the air gives coolness, (and) the rain is accompanied by the lightning. With this meaning of the whole text, we may search for its relevance in the Indus society. The statements indicate the very primitive state of the Indus society. Though the people were no more in the caves of the mountains, they had just begun to realise the values of the wealth of nature. But they were wise enough to propagate the knowledge gained by experience through these small inscriptions. The writing in India is as old as the human speech itself, slightly younger. Here we see the pulsating march of the humanity towards civilisation.

The language of the Indus texts is at the isolating stage and the same of the RV is at the inflexional stage in its typological development. This also corresponds to the thinking-pattern of the two communities. To the Indus people, the fire gives comfort through its warmth, the air gives coolness, and the rain comes with lightning. To the singers of the RV, the fire gives wealth. It is perhaps reminiscent of the age of urbanization and scientific developments when the fire used to produce precious things through chemical processes in the Indus society. Much later, in Gītā, the air is said to make something dry and the water is said to make something wet. The objects of nature were, more or less, the same, but the experiences of the people at two different epochs were remarkably different. That is why, the meanings of the Indus clauses and their fossilised forms in Vedic are comparable but hardly identical.

Even in the Meghadūta of Kālidāsa, the lightning accompanying the rain is supposed to show the path in the darkness of the night, but it can hardly be compared with the statement of the Indus texts. The monosyllabic words of the Indus language pointed to physical objects and crude thoughts, but at the third generation of the same language, when the Indus clauses had contracted into monosyllabic words, the thoughts had turned to be profound.

55

A Dry Reservoir of Water

na ta na ṣa ra

This little text is familiar to us through the three central signs for ta na ṣa. The sign for na at the beginning (from the right) and that for ra at the end (extreme left) have been newly introduced. They should have completely changed the context, so that the meaning of the already familiar ta na ṣa is no more the same. In a primitive language, the referends jump like frogs by a little shift in the context.

We know, the clause ta (womb) na (gem) ṣa (embryo) means: from the womb (of a woman) gems come out, which really refers to the birth of a child and which has phonetically fossilised as tánas in the RV (5, 70, 4), meaning 'an offspring'. Its further fossilization as tarṣ (tṛṣ) 'to be thirsty' in Vedic and its transportation to the Germanic languages (Eng. thirst, Germ. Durst) betrays an unpredictable shift in meaning. We, however, realise that 'the desire for a child' is a kind of thirst.

The same ta na ṣa is here preceded by na and followed by ra. The employment of a numeral sign for na perhaps shows that the two na have different meanings. This situation must have completely changed the meaning of the original clause ta na ṣa. The syllable na has a number of meanings in the Ekākṣarakoṣa. Let us take it in the usual sense of 'no, not'. If the <u>womb</u> for ta refers to some reservoir of waters, na naturally means <u>water</u>. The last syllable ra appears to be an affix for pluperfect, ṣa-ra then meaning 'had been'. Now the whole text seems to have the following meaning: the reservoir had no waters. The pluperfect idea is equa to a perfect continuous idea, indicating a long standing situation: there has been no water in the reservoir for a long time.

The text relates to Kalibangan, which might have been facing the shortage of waters for a long time. A grammarless language with monosyllabic words of the most primitive community is hardly more comprehensible than what we have guessed. We have no idea of what they needed and what were the natural impediments.

This text compels us to think that the same clause may have a different meaning in a different situation. The syllables preceding and following the main clause turns its meaning in an unpredictable direction. A monosyllabic word comprises a vast area of the meanings. As it extends by another syllable, the meaning is restricted, and this process goes on. We know, na is a 'river', but na-da is a 'river making indistinct noise', and na-d-ī is a 'large river'. Further, na-dá-nu is a 'thundering cloud', so that the original 'water' for na is gradually lost sight of.

56

The Origin of the Sāvitrī-stanza

The texts of the Indus inscriptions betray very primitive ideas, corresponding to the level of the civilisation then prevailing. It was the isolating and also the beginning of the agglutinative stage of the language: the words were monosyllabic (of the c-v type) and the grammatical element gha for future had just appeared. The people were probably at the beginning of the Neolithic age: they had given up hunting and gathering. The wandering (grā) had stopped (ma) and the founding of villages (grāma) was on anvil. Their suffering (da) too had ended (ma), and they were going to build houses (dama) for themselves. During this period, they had started agriculture through the help provided by the nature, although there are also references to the digging of canals and the carrying of waters from distant places.

They had been watching the behaviour of the nature, of the different seasons, and of the sun, responsible for them. It was at this stage of their social life that they wrote the inscription, ta gra ṣa ra gha 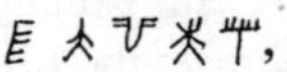, advising the people about the future course of action.

This text was taken up, first of all, in the 'Discovery of Indus' (1999) pp. 139-40, and then in the 'Evolution of the Indus language and its transition into Sanskrit' (2000) pp. 72-3. The meaning of the clause proposed there is not to be questioned, but the sublimation of the idea in the later ages is remarkable.

The initial meaning too was the result of a long experience of those primitive people. They were convinced that there was some relation between the summer and the flow of the waters in the river. As soon as the summer came, the rivers flowed with abundance of waters. They had also watched the relation between the hot summer and the rainy season.

The last syllable gha is the future affix, which suggests that the preceding ra (fire) is the verb. If it is transitive, the preceding ṣa (embryo/nipple) may be the object and gra (sun) preceding it may be the subject. But if gra is in the oblique case, ṣa itself may be the subject of some intransitive idea. The first syllable ta of the text appears to be adjective, meaning 'hot', qualifying the sun. Then the meaning of the clause is,

either
the hot sun will heat the embryo
or
by the hot sun the embryo will become hot.

The 'embryo' probably refers to 'the snow-clad Himalayas', the source of the fertilizing waters. The 'heating' also suggests the melting of the snow. At this stage of the language, much more is understood than what is actually said. Thus the clause seems to say: the hot sun will cause the snow to melt on the Himalayas and the river will flow with abundance of waters. Perhaps the people were advised to wait for the coming of the summer.

No identifiable Vedic word appears to be formed by the clustering of the syllables, but the ideas of the texts of the agglutinative stage continued to go forward. At the agglutinative stage itself, the verbal idea ra-gha (will heat/will become hot) turned into a verbal noun (light). Then the preceding ṣa became its adjective (brilliant). The whole clause became a phrase: the brilliant light of the hot sun. At the inflexional Vedic stage, when a 'filler' verb dhīmahi (we would receive) was brought to make a new sentence, the adjective 'hot' sublimated into 'divine' and 'brilliant' into 'inspiring': we would receive the inspiring light of the divine sun.

In the RV (3, 62, 10), it is the part of the famous Sāvitrī stanza with some editing in the original text:

tat savitur (gra) vareṇyaṃ (ṣa)
bhargo (ra) devasya (ta) dhīmahi.
(dhiyo yo naḥ pracodayāt).

As it is understood today, even dhīmahi has been sublimated into some mental activity (dhyāyema = let us think over).

The ideas expressed by the language at its first stage of development is naturally clumsy and rough, even vague. When the original idea was eclipsed at the next stage, a more cogent and sublime idea was imported. Thus we see that at the inflexional stage a typically primitive and pastoral idea is brought to a dizzy height. It is the daily prayer of a Brahmin in his religious life. What was originally the scorching rays of the hot sun changed into inspiration for the intellect (dhiyo yo naḥ pracodayāt).

57
Conclusion

A concluding chapter is out of place in this book, which is really the first part of the 'Early phase of the Indus civilisation'. The other parts may follow as and when the remaining texts are read and interpreted, either by myself or by some others.

A book like 'The mature phase of the Indus civilisation', revealed through the excavations and based on the texts, cannot be written unless the records of the agglutinative stage of the Indus language are discovered, almost ninety-nine per cent of which, written on perishable materials like palm-leaves, barks of the birch-trees, etc. are certainly lost. But some ten per cent of the same being the important documents of official nature, written on copper-plates, etc., must be there, lying near or far away from the old sites.

If the language of those texts agrees with the grammar reconstructed for the agglutinative stage of Indus, our idea of the linguistic embryology may vindicate. Then the linguistics will be a science like biology.

The ancient Indian history will have to be re-written, the Vedas will be interpreted more accurately and the Indian languages will have to be resurveyed dialect-wise regionally and level-wise socially. The racially conceived idea of the linguistic families will have to be dismantled.

Because the Indian culture is not a transplantation, its every item is rooted in the Indian soil. Only the unborn Brahmā knows when the Indian culture was born.